Sometimes
You Just Have
to Stand Naked

Sometimes You Just Have to Stand Naked

A GUIDE TO INTERESTING WRITING

David Bartholomy

Brescia College

Prentice-Hall, Inc., Englewood Cliffs, New Jersey 07632

Library of Congress Cataloging in Publication Data

Bartholomy, David
    Sometimes you just have to stand naked.

    1. College readers. 2. English language—Rhetoric.
I. Title.
PE1417.B374   808'.042   81–12731
ISBN 0–13–822593–1   AACR2

For George Gath

Cover and interior illustrations: Barney Saltzberg

© 1983 by Prentice-Hall, Inc., Englewood Cliffs, N.J. 07632

Printed in the United States of America

10 9 8 7 6 5 4 3 2 1

ISBN 0-13-822593-1

Prentice-Hall International, Inc., *London*
Prentice-Hall of Australia Pty. Limited, *Sydney*
Prentice-Hall Canada, Inc., *Toronto*
Prentice-Hall of India Private Limited, *New Delhi*
Prentice-Hall of Japan, Inc., *Tokyo*
Prentice-Hall of Southeast Asia Pte. Ltd., *Singapore*
Whitehall Books Limited, Wellington, *New Zealand*

NAKED CONTENTS

PREFACE TO THE INSTRUCTOR

I didn't want to write a preface for NAKED. I didn't see how I could possibly make it interesting.

"It doesn't have to be interesting," the editor argued. "People who read prefaces aren't looking for entertainment; they're looking for information."

"Can't we just tell them to read the instructor's manual?" I pleaded. "It has a preface. It even has an alternate table of contents written in normal textbook language."

"The book needs a preface," he insisted, "to help instructors decide whether to adopt it."

"But a preface won't fit in. Everything else in the book is for students."

I lost the argument, of course.

That evening I asked my students what they thought I should say in a preface to encourage other writing teachers to use my book.

"Tell them it's more like a friendly guide than a textbook," one suggested.

"Tell them it encourages people who don't consider themselves writers to open up and give it serious effort," another said.

"Tell them you've used it with your own students and it works."

"Tell them the samples are interesting to read as well as to the point."

"It's enjoyable to read. It's more like reading a novel than a textbook."

"It makes learning to write fun."

"I read the whole book the first week."

"Tell them their students will thank them for recommending it."

"Do I get royalties if you quote me?"

Lest you conclude from these statements that NAKED is merely interesting to read, let me assure you that I am as serious as I can be in this book about helping people write effectively. For that reason, I have included everything that I know will help them: explanations, perspectives, attitudes, tips, advice, writing suggestions, discussion and writing exercises, vocabularly exercises, style self-analyses, and samples of writing by students, professionals and myself. I've arranged it all in the order that has worked best in my own classes. And I've made it as interesting to read as I am able.

A basic theory behind NAKED is that what most students need in their first college writing course is to develop a positive attitude toward writing and confidence in their ability to do it effectively. To me, that means that they need to develop and refine their style more than they need to learn how to perform particular kinds of writing. After they have the attitude, the confidence and the style, they will be able to produce any kind of writing asked of them. I believe they are more likely to develop these qualities through personal experience writing than through the more objective forms such as analysis, criticism and research.

Thus in NAKED I cover matters of content and form—explaining and showing the value of using examples, of being detailed, of being thorough, of being organized—rather than explaining and prescribing the different writing modes. In chapters on style, analogies, diction and wordiness, I explain and show how to discover, refine and develop one's style. The thirty TIPS sprinkled through the text amount to a small handbook. A majority of the tips focus on stylistic irritants that appear in most inexperienced writers' styles.

I wrote NAKED to use as the main text in English 101. But, as I explain in the instructor's manual, it can be used in various ways in a variety of writing courses. It can be used alone or in conjunction with a handbook, a reader or a traditional rhetoric. It can function as the primary or secondary text or as supplementary reading not only in 101 but 102, advanced composition, creative writing, and even, I think, in basic English. Its value as the main text is that it is a self-contained writing course. Its value as a minor or supplementary text is the positive attitudes and motivation it generates as well as the information it offers, information that will help any student understand more clearly how to make his or her writing effective.

David Bartholomy

Sometimes You Just Have to Stand Naked

INTRO I

A Solitary Bird, Part I

It was 10:30 on a warm summer evening. The kids were asleep. Suzi was at work. I was sitting in the living room, listening to music and reading a novel.

The phone rang.

"Hello?"

"Hi, Bart. This is Scott."

"Oh, hi, Scott. How're you doing?"

"Okay. Hey, some of us are going skydiving a week from Sunday. You want to go along?"

"Skydiving? Uh, well . . . yeah, sure. Why not?"

I had been thinking about jumping out of an airplane for several years. But until that phone call I had figured it was something I'd never do. I was curious about what it would be like to float down in a parachute. But I was also afraid.

Afraid of rebreaking the leg that had taken over four years to heal the last time I broke it.

Afraid I'd kill myself.

But now I was committed. I'd said I'd do it, and I couldn't back out.

Then some calming thoughts occurred to me. Maybe it'll rain that day. Maybe I'll be sick. Maybe all the others will chicken out. (There were going to be eight of us, none of whom had jumped before.)

For the next ten days my emotions fluttered from curiosity to fear to hope; I wanted to do it . . . I was afraid to do it . . . I hoped I wouldn't have to . . . I wished it was all over.

Sunday dawned mostly cloudy and windy.

I thought, surely those guys won't want to drive all the way to Bardstown . . . just to be told the weather is too rough for jumping.

I was wrong.

(to be continued)

1

INTRO II

Life in the Woods

"C'mon, Grandpa. The sun's almost up."

"Well, let's go, then. Get in the car," said Grandpa as he rested his shotgun and Mark's new BB gun on the back seat.

Mark was quiet and thoughtful for most of the drive. Stubble fields, hay stacks, barns, cows, autumn woods ... all drifted through his vision practically unnoticed as Grandpa's big Oldsmobile floated through the early Indiana morning.

Grandpa was not as comfortable with the silence as Mark appeared to be. He wanted Mark to talk to distract him from his own confused thoughts.

"Well, Mark, how does it feel to be eight years old?"

"I dunno," said Mark after a few seconds. "I guess I feel older than eight."

"Yeah? How old do you feel?"

"Sort of like I've always been alive."

Grandpa reflected on the unconscious wisdom of youth, and sighed. "I know what you mean."

After a few more miles of silence, Mark asked, "Hey, Grandpa. Is there anything in Uncle Grover's woods besides squirrels?"

"Sure," said Grandpa, his mood beginning to lift. "There's birds, garter snakes, mice, a stray cow now and then."

"Is that all?"

"That's all you're likely to see. But it's not all that's there, not by any means. The woods are full of creatures that most people have never seen or heard of. Some can disguise themselves to look like anything they want: a twig, a floating leaf, a puddle, a spot of sun on the grass."

"Really?"

"Sure." Grandpa paused a moment, then added, "Boy, I can see you've got a lot to learn about life in the woods."

Suddenly Mark pointed and said, "Hey, wasn't that Uncle Grover's farm?"

Grandpa tromped on the brake, throwing them both forward and sending the car skidding on the gravel.

As they drove up Grover's lane, Mark felt himself moving into the presence of some undefined adventure. At the end of the lane, Grandpa stopped, then started backing across the yard toward the house. Mark was looking out the windshield at the receding field of dried corn stalks when the car stopped with a jerk and a thud.

"Grandpa!"

"You boys all right?"

Mark looked toward the voice and saw his great-uncle Grover, Grandpa's brother, rocking on bowed legs across the yard, a worried smile on his cracked leather face.

"Jeez, Gus," said Grover, "this car's got dents all over it. You been drivin' in demo derbies?"

"Naw. My garage door shrunk," said Grandpa. "Sorry I barked your tree."

"Oh, you didn't hurt the tree, just your bumper."

"Well, what's one more dent? You got any coffee?"

"Sure. C'mon in the house. Onie's in the kitchen."

As they walked up onto the porch and into the house, Grover asked, "By the way, Gus, why were you backing across the yard?"

"The yard?" Grandpa looked puzzled for a second, then began to smile. "Well, maybe it's time you moved that driveway, anyway. Might as well put it where it'll be used."

When they entered the kitchen, Mark's great-aunt Onie was bent at the waist, her head in the oven and her wide hips in the air. Grandpa patted her affectionately and said, "Cookies! Lady, you're always baking something good. Mind if I try one?"

"You just help yourself, Gus. You, too, Mark. My, look how you've grown. You're getting to be as tall and good-looking as your Grandpa there. Ain't he, Grover."

"Sure he is. So you're goin' huntin', eh, boy?"

"Yemf," Mark answered through a mouthful of sugar cookies.

Onie smiled and said, "Well, that should make a nice birthday. Here, take this sack of cookies along—a little present from me."

"Thanks," Mark said. "You ready, Grandpa?"

"Just let me finish this coffee."

To speed things up, Mark walked out on the porch. Looking around the familiar barnyard, he smiled when he saw the fat white chickens, running and clucking stupidly. But the smile faded as he remembered what the chickens would look like later: spattering the grass with blood, their feet lashed to a clothesline, jerking headless.

(to be continued)

INTRO III

Here I Go Again

During the first several years I taught this course, I tried several different books. But I finally realized that, for me, teaching with someone else's book is as uncomfortable as wearing someone else's Levi's.

So, seven years ago I decided to try writing my own. But, like so many other things I've decided to do, I knew that I would put it off forever unless I could find some way to force myself to do it. Finally, I decided simply not to order a book for class that fall. Then I would either have to face my students empty-handed or give them something of my own.

I jotted down ideas and outlines off and on through that summer. But when the school year was about to begin, I didn't have one page written. And I was kicking myself for not just ordering a book in the first place. Then, the night before the first class, I panicked and wrote an introduction. And each week after that I wrote a new chapter.

The students seemed to enjoy the idea of their teacher writing his own book, probably because they knew I was suffering the same torture they were. But even before the course was finished, I could tell from the quality of their writing that the book hadn't helped them as much as I'd wanted it to.

So I decided to try again. Suzi had begun working evenings at the local newspaper, and we figured we could afford to forgo my usual summer occupations, teaching summer school and supervising a playground. I would use the time instead to rewrite the book. I had several ideas, and I was excited about the project. As it turned out, though, I was more excited about going swimming with the kids (Bridget was 7, Matt 6, and Jude 4½), playing golf, canoeing, reading, playing tonk down at the tavern and listening to music. It was a good summer. But when the end of August arrived, I hadn't even begun rewriting the book. So I repeated the first year's pattern, bringing in a piece to the class as I wrote it each week.

When the semester was over I was more satisfied with the book than I'd been a year earlier, but it still wasn't as effective as I wanted it to be. So the next year, and the next, I wrote it again . . . and began to think of it as an endless project, as much a part of my autumn as pumpkins and football.

Then, last year, I made up my mind to write it well enough that I wouldn't mind using it more than once. After all, I told myself, there's a lot to do in autumn besides write a textbook.

Well, last year's version was the best yet. It still wasn't as effective as I wanted it to be, but I thought it was good enough to send off to some publishers to see what they thought of it. They thought it was ". . . witty, engaging, and totally unique . . . but too idiosyncratic."

So, here I go again. It's the night before the first class. . . .

INTRO IV

Nuts to Anything That's Not Interesting

Ed: Wait a minute! First you begin a skydiving story, then a story about some kid going hunting, then the history of this book. What's going on?

[*Reader:*   The voice you just heard belongs to Ed. He's my writing conscience, formed by all the conventional, unimaginative teachers I've been unable to ignore. His approach to writing is conservative, coat and tie; my own is jeans and shirt-sleeves. Maybe together we can control my "idiosyncratic" tendencies and produce a book that is both interesting and effective.]

Me: Ed, I'm just trying to abide by one of the first rules of writing: The beginning must somehow interest the readers enough to make them want to read on. I thought a triple beginning might be interesting.

Ed: It's interesting enough, but it's confusing.

Me: It'll become clear.

Ed: But why not just write the usual introduction—explain what the book's about?

Me: Because it wouldn't be interesting. And NUTS to. . . .

Ed: I know. I know. I've heard your nutshell philosophy before: "Nuts to anything that's not interesting."

Me: That's right. Especially writing. To be effective, writing must be interesting from the start and maintain that interest throughout. If it isn't interesting, it doesn't deserve to be read . . . and it usually won't be.

Ed: You'd better be careful. You're climbing out onto a limb from which you might end up hanging yourself. Correct me if I'm mistaken, but what I hear you saying is that *all* writing should be interesting.

Me: That's right.

Ed: But that's saying even textbooks should be interesting, and that means. . . .

Me: I know. . . .

Ed: . . . even *your* writing, your *textbook*, has to be interesting.

Me: Look, Ed. If I can't make my own writing interesting, how can I presume to tell other people how to make theirs interesting?

Ed: I agree. And I even agree that it may be possible to write a textbook that's interesting. But I'm not sure you're the one to do it. You did say this is your eighth attempt, didn't you?

Me: Practice makes perfect?

Ed: Maybe so. But if you want my opinion, you're off to a shaky start.

Me: Yeah, well, there's always next year.

INTRO V

What's Interesting?

Hello, Reader. What I'm going to attempt with this book is to help you realize that you have many interesting things to write about, and that you can write about them in ways that people who read what you've written will find interesting.

Of course, the big question is, What makes writing interesting? It's going to take this whole book for me to answer that question. I will say this here, though: Interesting writing is a blend of an interesting subject, an appropriate form and an interesting style.

Finding interesting subjects is easy enough; just write about those things *you* find interesting, exciting, pleasurable, funny, sad . . . anything that arouses your emotions . . . anything about which you feel.

An appropriate form is one that suits your subject, your purpose and your audience, and that sets limits within which you can function effectively.

An interesting style is one that is clear, confident, honest, individual, colorful, precise. Not necessarily one that makes you laugh or cry, but certainly one that makes you want to read on.

Read on.

INTRO VI

Some Good Advice

The ideal audience for most of the writing I'll ask you to do is a segment of the general public that is interested in what you are interested in. When you do these writings, write as if for publication in a magazine which people like you read.

Make the most of each assignment. Go beyond what it asks for. Personalize it. If you do this, you won't write as if you're answering a question or fulfilling an assignment. Instead, you'll be detailed, honest, interesting.

Realize that the more detailed your writing is, the more likely you are to be understood. Your goal should be complete communication, regardless of length.

Write about what you care about. And care about what you write.

SOMETIMES YOU JUST HAVE TO STAND NAKED

INTRO VII

Why Write?

Writing is hard work. It can also be satisfying, even fun. And it's a worthwhile skill to develop, whether or not you have dreams of becoming a writer. Improving your writing skills will make you a better student, and it will make much of your college work easier and more enjoyable. It will make more jobs available to you when you're out of school. It will also make you a better reader . . . less tolerant of poor writing and more appreciative of effective writing. And it will develop your mind and your ability to communicate what's on it.

There are fringe benefits, too. As a result of the writing you'll do in this course, you will experience an increase in self-awareness. In addition, you'll be more aware of the complexity and beauty of the world around you. And, if all goes well, you will be more confident, not only of your ability to communicate in writing, but more confident in general.

And you'll be a more interesting person.

I think these are important benefits. I hope you experience even more.

Ed: *Seven* introductions?

Me: What's wrong with that?

Ed: Well, why stop there? Why not eight, ten, eighteen? You've already rendered the idea of an introduction meaningless.

Me: Ed, why do you feel threatened by things just because they're unconventional? Relax. Life's more interesting when you open yourself to new possibilities.

WRITING EXERCISE _____

Introduce yourself to, and begin conversing with, another person in the class. First become comfortable with each other. Then learn all you can about the other person's likes and dislikes, ambitions, interests, hopes, fears, etc. Dig, dig, dig. This is an interesting and unique person. Find out what it is that makes him or her interesting and unique.

Then answer all the other person's questions about you, thoroughly and honestly. Tell him or her all about yourself . . . what you're like now and how you came to be this way. Concentrate on what's most interesting about you. Relax and be yourself.

When you're both satisfied that you know each other well enough, write about this person. Write for an audience that has never seen the other person and doesn't know anything about him or her. Either write a general profile, showing everything that makes this person interesting, or concentrate on and show the one aspect of this person that most interests you.

Make it an accurate profile. Quote the other person so your readers can hear what he or she sounds like and what he or she has to say. Describe the person so they can see what he or she looks like. Give them something specific to remember. Be honest. Tell the truth, as you see it, about this person.

Write the profile as if for publication in the college newspaper or some national publication with readers who would be interested in this person.

Note: There is no "right" way to write this sort of thing. Do it any way that seems to you to be interesting and effective.

SOMETIMES YOU JUST HAVE TO STAND NAKED

College
is a
mental institution!

CHAPTER 1

on the road

A Solitary Bird, Part II

Ahead of us on the interstate, Randy was engaging in one of his favorite activities: high-speed driving. His two passengers, Scott and Jack, were entertaining themselves taking pictures. Both were reporters from the local newspaper, and they were planning a feature story on our skydiving adventure. I hoped it would have a happy ending.

The driver of the car I was riding in, Danny, was determined to keep up with his brother Randy. A couple of wired-up electricians, they were both enthusiastic about going skydiving. Danny's less enthusiastic passengers were Glen, with whom I used to tend bar occasionally; Gary, another reporter; and me, a nervous English teacher.

Kula, the "Outdoors Editor" at the newspaper, was somewhere behind us, accompanied by his wife and two kids. I had discouraged Suzi and our kids from coming along. I didn't want them to witness my shame if I should give in to my fears . . . which were mounting steadily as we drove further and further from home.

One thing I noticed about fear that morning: it's a great source of hope. I found myself hoping that something, anything—rain, wind, even a minor automobile accident—would intervene and save me from having to jump.

Another thing I noticed about fear is that it doesn't do much for conversation, and it makes humor almost impossible. It's a tremendous stimulus for thought, though, and the lack of conversation in our car left me plenty of time and freedom to indulge all the thoughts my brain insisted on punishing me with. Unfortunately, most of them were about fear.

11

The more I thought about it, the more it became clear that I was really suffering from three fears at once: fear of the unknown, fear of inadequacy, and fear of danger (including death). None of them were strangers to me, though I couldn't recall ever before having experienced all three simultaneously.

I've experienced fear of the unknown almost everytime I've approached a new situation, like beginning at a new school, or getting married.

Fear of inadequacy is equally familiar. I've felt it, for example, on my first day of teaching and on my first try at waterskiing. And I feel it with each new attempt to write this book.

But those two fears were gentle breezes compared to the hurricane that was wasting what remained of my composure: fear of danger. My most memorable previous experience of this fear was in conjunction with my first canoe trip. Four of us were about to embark on a small river in eastern Kentucky. I had never canoed before in my life, much less on water with rapids in it. And I had just read James Dickey's novel *Deliverance*, about murderous rapids and murderous people encountered by four city men canoeing a small river in the South. As a result, I was subjecting myself to a battery of negative thoughts . . . such as being dashed against huge boulders and drowned . . . or being painfully and viciously murdered by nine-fingered hillbillies.

Fortunately, I had enough sense left to recall that most of these previous fears had been unnecessary. I made it through grade school, high school, college and graduate school; I'm happy with our marriage; I think waterskiing is a trip; I haven't given up on writing this book; and I've been canoeing small rivers in the South a few times a year since that first excursion. I'm alive, unhurt and better in many ways for having faced all those "frightening" situations rather than backing out. I've learned that fear is usually irrational, groundless and natural, and that it shouldn't be allowed to interfere with something I want to do.

On the other hand, I recalled, I had never jumped out of an airplane . . . a half-mile high . . . with only a piece of cloth to prevent me from being converted into an unrecognizable glob of blood and broken bones.

(to be continued)

WHAT YOU CAN DO WITH YOUR THOUGHTS

The thoughts on fear in the few paragraphs I've just written are not unlike many entries in my journals. They are analytic, picking apart experiences and feelings in an attempt to understand them, and therefore to understand myself.

Why is he talking about journals? you ask yourself nervously. You already know the answer.

I want YOU to begin keeping one. Which leads naturally to the question: What is a journal?

First, a journal is not the same thing as a diary. When I think of a diary, I think of thirteen-year-old girls keeping a record of their unrequited loves and other passions. "He looked at me today!! I was so excited I almost fainted!" (I don't know where I picked up the idea that girls do that. It must be a stereotype from the movies.)

A *diary* chronicles and comments on events and experiences. A *journal* is a record of the working of one's mind. If you write about what you did, you're keeping a diary. If you write about what you thought (and are thinking), you're keeping a journal.

ON LOVE, LIMITS, AND LIFE

I've been flipping through a journal I was keeping a few years ago. Most of the entries were made late at night, with the kids in bed and Suzi at work. And most of them began with nothing particular in mind, though what came out were usually matters that had been on my mind sometime during the day. I would put on some records, open a beer, make myself comfortable, open the journal and begin writing whatever came into my head.

Here's an entry whose origin I'm uncertain about. I was probably trying to reconcile that feeling I have at times that my responsibilities are limiting my freedom.

> When you wake up in the morning, remind yourself to have the best time you can . . . doing things you want to do as well as the things you have to do to fulfill your commitment to the people you love. It's the only chance you'll have to live this day. Make it one you'll remember for all the good you accomplished and all the love you showed. . . .

> Recognize and accept the limits that result from the commitments. There is abundant freedom within those limits, once you accept them. Until you accept them, you'll be unsettled, needlessly. (Love is freedom . . . and freedom can only come with love. Without it, there is an emptiness which imprisons the would-be-free soul.)

That entry illustrates two characteristics of journal writing: (1) You don't have to make sense to anyone but yourself; and (2) you can be as sappy and sentimental as you like.

Here are some other entries from that journal.

> People are taught from birth a particular view of reality . . . and are so brainwashed that they'll defend that view to the death rather than admit there may be other equally valid views.

The mind *creates* order . . . because it's been taught to fear chaos.

Don't be afraid of failure. You learn and grow by pushing out your limits . . . by doing what you're not sure you *can* do.

If you surrender to fear . . . whether it's fear of the unknown or fear of your own inadequacy . . . you accept unnecessary and restricitve limits. If, instead, you disregard fear and meet the challenge head-on, you destroy the illusion of limits. And you grow, in confidence and perspective.

Truth is illusive/elusive. You have it in your head, but before you can capture it on paper it slips away just enough that it's no longer what you were thinking. And it's no longer the truth. Truth is unwilling to be caught and held. Which is to say that truth is constantly changing. It's moving and you're trying to stamp some label on it. Even if you hit it, the truth that you label is already false, or at most a semblance of truth. Your best bet is to just keep your eye on it (truth). Use it as a guide rather than as matter to be communicated. Each of us must discover his or her own truth, anyway. Each person must be allowed to create his or her own dream. That's the truth. Thus fiction writers (and all other writers who attempt to portray life truthfully) are more effective than the philosophers. They create symbols of truth, rather than attempting to label it. As truth changes, so does the meaning of the symbol.

Kids are more interesting than adults. Once you start hanging around and tuning in on kids, adults with all their games, hang-ups, selfishness, problems, and "ate-up" values seem hardly worth your attention. This is not absolutely true, of course. Even so, the more interesting adults are the more child-like ones.

The more imaginative and less "straight" (normal, typical) something is . . . including writing . . . the more interesting it is.

Remember to mention the need for and value of being honest in writing. Honesty is born of trust . . . but can also beget it. Dishonesty with self begets dishonesty with others. And vice versa.

"The times you impress me the most are the times when you don't try."
                                                                    Joni Mitchell

        Don't use those entries of mine as any more than the most general example of what to write in your journal. What *I* write reflects the way my mind works—and therefore the person I am. What ends up in your journal should be an accurate reflection of *you*. Use your journal to record your observations, insights, ideas, thoughts, opinions, feelings, lines from songs and poems, anything that makes sense . . . or attempts to make sense . . . of your life.

HELP FOR THE FORGETFUL

Why keep a journal? Well, for one reason, because we tend to forget most of the valuable results of our mental activity if we don't record them. I wish I knew some of what was going through my mind on February 19, 1966. But I don't, and I never will because I kept no record. I know what I was doing that day but not what I was thinking. And the only reason I remember anything at all of the day is because it's the day I was married. Less meaningful days, August 14, 1971, for example, are lost to me completely.

Another reason for keeping a journal is so that you'll know yourself better. Without a record (or a photographic memory), most of what you were and most of what's gone into the process of your becoming who you are today is lost. (How can you know who you are if you don't know where you've come from?)

I think these are good reasons for keeping a journal. And there are lots more. But *my* main reason for suggesting that you keep one is because I know that doing it will help you develop two very important writing assets: (1) your natural writing style . . . a voice that sounds like you and no one else; and (2) openness and honesty in communication. When you write in your journal, you'll write knowing that no one but yourself need ever read what you've written. Thus, you can say *what* you want (openness) . . . and you can say it the *way* you want (natural style).

And there's one more important reason for keeping a journal: Writing in it is likely to give you good ideas for interesting subjects that you can develop into major writings later.

Eventually, what's going on in your journal will affect everything else that you write. Your writing will all be increasingly honest, individualized, self-confident . . . and, therefore, interesting.

IT CAN'T HURT YOU

Select a notebook for your journal which is easy to carry but which is not so small that it discourages you from writing lengthy entries. A 6-by-9½-inch notebook is a good size.

It should be easy to carry so that you can keep it with you wherever you are. There's no telling when you might have something to write in it. Thoughts come unpredictably, and if they're not recorded immediately they're usually lost forever.

If you come to the end of the day without having made any entries, sit down then and write something, even if it's only a recap of the day. At least the day won't be lost to you. You might want to do this at the end of every day, anyway.

Keeping a journal has to become a habit. For this reason, it's essential that you write something in it every day, no matter how inconvenient it might seem. If you skip one day, pretty soon you'll be skipping two, then a week, then. . . .

Try it for a few weeks before deciding whether it's something you want to continue. It can't hurt you.

WRITING EXERCISE _____

Buy a journal notebook today. Begin writing in it immediately. Make at least one lengthy entry a day.

FROM PRIVATE TO PUBLIC

I said a little bit ago that journal writing can produce interesting subjects for major writings. The story that follows was born in one of Beth Lindsey's early journal entries. It remained in her journal for most of the semester, until she had learned enough about writing that she was able to see how she could write about the experience effectively.

Her Majesty, My Sister
Beth Chilton Lindsey

When you have an older sister who is pretty, popular and two years ahead of you in school, you almost get used to not having an identity of your own. When three out of four teachers think of you as "Felicity Ward's little sister," and four out of four boys only notice you as a means to an end (Felicity, or Phil, as I call her), the slings and arrows of outrageous fortune blunt a little bit after awhile.

I mean, you never stop wishing you were just Stephanie Ward (or Stevie, as I'm used to being called), a person in your own right, instead of a satellite caught in the orbit of a brighter planet; but eventually, as the years wear on, you accept the inevitable and try to live with it.

Yet nothing is ever so bad that it can't get worse, as I found out the year the first Miss Teen Henry County contest was held.

It all started one grim afternoon in January when we drove home with one of the members of Phil's fan club.

Phil sat in the front seat, every honey-colored hair obediently in place. I sat in the back seat, a refugee from last period gym (with five minutes to change from gym suit to clothes), hair hanging like limp spaghetti and perspiring wherever it is that you perspire when you want to look cool and unruffled.

"Did you see the thing about the Miss Teen Henry County Contest?" asked Phil's current chauffeur.

"No, I didn't," Phil said.

"It was on the bulletin board outside the lunchroom. There's an entry form you have to use. I picked one up for you."

"Oh, Frank, how thoughtful of you," Phil purred. "But what's it all about?"

"It's a contest to pick Miss Teen Henry County. It says something like she should be a representative of all the good things that characterize the younger generation. A shining example of youth, vitality, healthy good looks, talent and school involvement. Something like that."

Something like that! He'd memorized the whole stupid thing to recite to Phil. Frank is really subtle.

"You really ought to enter," he said. "You'd win for sure."

"Oh, I don't know," Phil said modestly. (She can afford to sound modest, since she has absolutely nothing to sound modest about.)

"No, honestly," Frank persisted, "I think you should try. Don't you think so, Stevie?"

Startled that he would bother talking to the serf when the queen was around, I wasn't ready for Frank's question.

"Huh?" I asked cleverly.

"Don't you think Felicity owes it to herself to enter the contest?"

"Oh, yes, definitely. Absolutely. Phil owes it to herself. To her parents, too; to the whole community, as a matter of fact."

Phil turned around to give me a dirty look.

"That's a good point," Frank went on, blithely unaware of any tinge of sarcasm. "You do owe it to us all," he said. "Think of what it would do for the school if you became Miss Teen Henry County."

"Rah, rah," I murmured.

"Think of your parents, how proud they'd be; and Stevie. Wouldn't you be proud, Stevie?"

"Hysterically," I agreed.

"Think of the kids in school, your friends, your teachers. . . ."

"Think of the starving children in Europe," I offered.

Phil whipped her head around and peered at me through dangerously narrowed eyes. Frank pulled up in front of the house.

"Here," he said, digging a slip of paper out of his pocket. "At least take an entry form and look it over. What have you got to lose?"

"All right," Phil conceded, rewarding Frank with one of her toothpaste commercial smiles. "If you think I should."

Frank beamed. We lumbered out of the car. I lumbered, that is; Phil flowed gently, like honey.

"Thanks for the ride, Frank," she said.

"Any time," he replied eagerly.

"What a dope," I mumbled as he pulled away.

"Frank?" Phil said vaguely, scanning the entry blank in her hand. "Oh, Frank's all right."

"Yeah? For what?" I demanded, trudging up the front steps.

My mother and father were unanimously agreed that Phil must make her own decision about entering the contest.

"We don't want to influence you at all," my mother explained, "because once you decide what you're going to do, you have to live with the decision. It would be exciting, though. . . ."

"Now, what your mother means," said my father, "is that there can be an awful lot of pressure in a competition like this. Of course, you've always worked very well under pressure. . . ."

"But it's entirely up to you," my mother reminded her. "I can't wait to tell Aunt Geraldine. . . ."

"So don't feel that we're pushing you in one direction or another," my father went on. "What would you do for the talent contest?"

Thus did my sister make her own decision, voluntarily, without duress or influence, and of her own free will.

That evening we all sat around the kitchen table to help Phil fill out the entry form. In addition to the usual things like name, address, age, etc., it had a few zingies that really hung us up for a while.

"Why I like to live in Henry County," Phil read out loud.

"Who thought that one up?" I asked.

"The chamber of commerce," she said.

"Oh. Okay, how about this: Picturesque Henry County, conveniently situated midway between Carrollton and Louisville, named after the famous patriot Patrick Henry, with an average mean temperature of three degrees below zero. . . ."

"Come on," Phil snapped, "stop kidding around."

"Don't you think that's chamber of commerce type stuff?" I asked innocently.

Phil frowned and made some notes on a piece of scrap paper.

"Listen," she said triumphantly. "I like living in Henry County because it combines the charm of a small town with the facilities of a bustling metropolis. Retaining the best of the rural atmostphere while offering the advantages of urban life, Henry County manages to keep one foot in the country and the other in the city."

"Henry County's going to end up with a charley horse," I commented.

"That's pretty good," my father commented, "except for the part about the feet."

"How about 'Henry County manages to have the best of both worlds'?" Phil asked.

"Fine," my mother said. "Perfect."

Then it asked for two teacher references, and Phil couldn't figure out which teachers to put down.

"But they'd all say nice things about you," my mother said.

"That's the problem," Phil groaned. "I don't know who to pick. They all like me."

"The rest of us should have such problems," I sympathized.

After we cleared that hurdle, there was the question of what Phil would do in the talent competition.

"You could sing," my father suggested.

SOMETIMES YOU JUST HAVE TO STAND NAKED

"Or do one of those dances," my mother said.

"You could recite 'The Boy Stood on the Burning Deck' with dramatic gestures," I contributed.

My sister glared, which was okay, since being ignored was getting on my nerves.

They finally decided that she would sing and dance, since a double threat always impresses the judges of these things.

Then there was the space for listing extracurricular activities. Would you believe that Phil's problem there was that the space wasn't big enough to fit all hers in?

"Why don't you just attach an extra sheet of paper with the things you didn't have room for on the form?" my mother suggested.

"Or just put down the important ones," my father said.

"But they're all important!" Phil insisted.

"Why don't you just write, 'I belong to everything and am the president of almost everything'?" I said.

"Stephanie, you sound almost hostile!" my mother chided.

"Me? Hostile? Why in the world would I be hostile?"

"Could it be that you're a little jealous of your sister?" my father asked gently.

A little? No, not a little!

"We're proud of both of you," he went on, his voice brimming with paternal reassurance.

"Why, of course we are!" said my mother, sounding actually shocked that this might be a matter of doubt.

I shrugged as if I didn't care. I didn't believe them, to tell you the truth, but it was nice to know that they were worried about it.

There are two high schools in Henry County; there is Henry County High, which we attend, and Henry County Low (as we call it, but it is actually our sister school called Eminence High School).

We didn't know how many girls from Henry County Low were competing in the contest, but five girls from our school had entered, and it was the consensus that Phil was the front runner.

Even Regina Clubb, one of the other contestants, admitted to me that she didn't know why she bothered.

"Who's going to beat your sister? If it wasn't that my mother wasn't once Miss Henry County Fair, I wouldn't be in this thing at all."

And at home, things were pretty frantic. In between listening to Phil rehearse to "Spinning Wheel," my mother sewed her costume and tried to judge whether Phil's dance would be improved by the addition of a little baton twirling, which also happens to be one of Phil's specialties.

And in the meantime, all the feelings of inferiority I always had now had the glorious opportunity to take over completely. I wasn't just Felicity Ward's little sister anymore; I was now Felicity Ward the future Miss Teen Henry County's little sister. And wasn't I proud to be Felicity Ward's little sister?

I can't begin to tell you. . . .

The day of the contest finally arrived, and cool, calm Felicity was a nervous wreck. Would you believe she couldn't find her baton (she'd decided on a triple threat), and she broke down and cried? Eventually, though, she got herself together, and we left for the Henry County Civic Auditorium at 10:00 A.M. The contest didn't start till two, but they wanted to have a couple of run-throughs so everyone would know in what order things would happen, and so the girls would have a chance to rehearse with the combo they'd hired to accompany anyone who needed accompanying.

When we got there, the place was swarming with subdued contestants and vocal mothers. There was also an oversupply of little sisters who paraded up and down the stage for vicarious thrills and ran shrieking from little brothers who chased them up and down the aisles of the auditorium.

"Are you nervous?" I asked Phil solicitously.

She gave me one of her withering looks.

By now I was beginning to be nervous, and for the very first time since Phil had entered this thing, I could honestly feel unjealous. Abject feelings of relief bobbed through me as I watched thirteen flustered girls trying to follow directions from the M.C., the contestant director and their mothers.

It was hot and stuffy in the auditorium. By one o'clock, what few fingernails I'd had that morning were but a ragged memory, and my hair was falling lankly over my face like a sodden veil. Heat, tension and a slow, creeping boredom combined to overwhelm me, and I felt myself slipping into a groggy stupor.

At last my lethargy was interrupted as people began filling seats in the auditorium. The decibel level grew, the excitement mounted, and promptly at two thirty-five, the two o'clock show got under way.

I looked around for my parents, but they were up front somewhere, probably looking around for Aunt Margaret and Uncle Charlie, Aunt Betty and Uncle Jerry, Cousin Louise-from-Louisville and several dozen other people they had asked to come.

"Hello, everyone, and welcome to the First Annual Miss Teen Henry County Contest. I'm your master of ceremonies, Brian Young, and I want to tell you that the tension is really building here, because backstage thirteen lovely young ladies are waiting for. . . ."

Then he introduced the president of the chamber of commerce who made a brief speech approximately the length of *War and Peace*. During this there was a disturbance in my aisle as a boy squeezed past knees and stepped on feet, working his way toward the empty seat on my right.

The M.C. introduced the combo as "Russ Jones and the Denim Blues" and then sang a song with them called, so help me, "Miss Teen Henry County, Our Teenage Queen." This song was written, of course, by the wife of the president of the chamber of commerce!

I tried to look at the boy next to me without turning my head. He seemed to be about my age and sort of nice looking. Strangely, he was listening intently to the song and did not appear nauseated by it, which immediately gave me doubts about his sanity.

Finally, the real action got under way.

All the contestants walked out on the stage and were introduced one by one. Each apparently had brought along her cheering section, and as her

SOMETIMES YOU JUST HAVE TO STAND NAKED

name was called, each girl smilingly acknowledged the screams, whistles and cheers of her little brothers, sisters and less inhibited relatives.

Phil was fifth, and as she was introduced I felt myself actually shaking with excitement.

I applauded wildly and heard someone yell "YAY" in a shrill voice. When I realized it was my own voice, I shriveled down in my seat, feeling like a dumb little kid.

"And how old are you, Felicity?" Brian Young asked.

"Eighteen," Phil replied calmly.

The boy on my right was staring at me; I could feel it, even though my eyes were riveted on Phil. I grew uncomfortable and self-conscious, and I was irritated because I just wanted to worry about what was happening to my sister. Finally I couldn't stand it anymore. When they went on to the next girl, I turned to him, and, sure enough, he was eyeing me.

"That was my sister," I explained.

"No kidding?" he said, his face suddenly alive with interest.

"No kidding," I said dully. It usually happened this way; one glimpse of Phil was a fatal dose.

"She's pretty," he said, which was the understatement of the week.

"Yeah, I know." I suppose even now I couldn't help the bitterness.

"That's my brother," he said abruptly.

"Who?" I asked, startled. "Brian Young?"

"No. Russ Jones. With the guitar. That's his group."

I took a good look at the guitarist. He didn't resemble this guy at all. He was your classic blond, tall and handsome, oozing self-assurance.

"He's good," I said, meaning it.

"I know," the boy replied glumly. "He always was." His tone sounded strangely familiar.

They finally got to the talent competition. Phil was scheduled to go on next-to-last, and I sat through a tap dance, a cello solo, several songs and two twirling routines. Neither baton twirler was as good as Phil, I noted with relief, and one of them dropped her baton twice.

When Phil started her performance, I was so tense that I was gripping the arms of the seat and clenching my teeth. She looked fantastic; my mother had made her a white and silver dress that flowed as she moved, making her look like some kind of angel.

She sang beautifully, danced gracefully and didn't drop her baton once. I don't think I breathed at all until she raised her arms triumphantly, bowed low, and acknowledged the applause with a radiant smile (that was probably relief as much as anything else).

"She's really good," the boy next to me said. I exhaled and began to uncurl my fingers from the arm rest. They were stiff and my jaw ached.

"Do you do that stuff, too?" he asked.

"No," I sighed, too weak to cringe at the comparison between Phil and me.

"I can't even carry a tune," he confided. "My brother has all the talent in our family."

No wonder his tone of voice had sounded familiar when he talked about his brother! That must be what I sounded like when I mentioned Phil. Here was a guy after my own heart.

He smiled a nice, warm smile. "Believe me," I said, "I know exactly how you feel."

"I'll bet you do," he agreed. "By the way, my name is John."

"Mine's Stev . . . I mean Stephanie! But you can call me Stevie."

The talent part of the program was over; all that was left was an "informal chat" with the contestants.

Brian Young asked Phil, "What is important to you in life?"

This, I thought, is an informal chat?

"People," Phil said smoothly, as if that were the most obvious thing in the world.

"People are what life is all about. You can't walk through life alone, so it's important to be able to get along with others, to use all your understanding and compassion and love in dealing with everyone you meet. I can't think of anything more important than that."

Atta girl, Phil!

Applause, applause and a loud bass cheer, which tipped me off that Uncle Jerry was somewhere in the audience.

The boy next to me leaned over and whispered, "When she wins let's introduce her to my brother."

"Good idea," I agreed. "But don't jump to any conclusions yet."

But I didn't see how she could lose.

"And now for the Big Moment!" Brian Young cried. "While the judges are making their decision, ladies and gentlemen, Russ Jones and the Denim Blues will provide us with some entertainment."

"Brian Young's a real swinger himself," John murmured.

"Oh, yeah," I said cynically.

That was all that was said, though. For the next few minutes I couldn't open my mouth; I couldn't shift positions in my seat. I didn't even know if my pulse was pulsing.

"Do you think they'll do the fourth runner-up, third runner-up bit?" John wondered.

"Mpf," I replied, between clenched teeth.

"You're probably right," he said with a smile.

"Ladies and gentlemen! The judges have made their decision! I want you to meet the First Miss Teen Henry County . . ."

Come on, you refugee from Atlantic City, you pseudo-swinger, you suburban Bert Parks, you. . . .

"Felicity Ann Ward!!!"

I screamed. I definitely, unashamedly, wholeheartedly screamed.

The applause was not exactly deafening, but Phil had a good contingent of friends and relatives to keep it going while she was crowned.

There was, however, one nine-year-old, male "BOO!" from the audience.

"Sore loser," John sneered, clapping almost as loudly as I was.

They were crowning Phil with something tiaralike and sparkling, and I found that everything suddenly blurred because there were, of all ridiculous things, tears in my eyes.

"Hey," John said, shaking my arm, "let's go congratulate your sister."

"Okay," I agreed.

"Then let's go get something to eat. I have a feeling we have a lot in common."

"Little siblings of the world, unite. . . ." I mumbled, not expecting him to hear me.

"You have nothing to lose but your rivalry," he shot back, as we worked our way out of the aisle.

He turned and smiled at me. Together we struggled forward to reach his brother and my sister.

Afterthoughts

When I first told Beth I enjoyed that story, she was surprised. She said she'd been having trouble writing a story she cared a lot more about, and she had decided to write this one instead just to see if she could write a story "like the ones you read in magazines." I realized while I was reading it that it was a formula "sibling rivalry" story, but, like I told Beth, it's far better than most, thanks to Beth's obvious understanding of Stevie's feelings, her understanding of how to tell a story, her humor and the clarity of her language. Which, not accidentally, leads to the last thing I want to talk about before ending this chapter.

A WORD A DAY KEEPS CONFUSION AWAY

All of us have a tendency to use the same few words over and over, whether they're exactly accurate or not. That's not a problem when you're writing to yourself in your journal. It's not much of a problem when you're talking, either. (The listener can always say "Huh?") It is a problem when you're writing something others are going to read, though, because you're not going to be there to answer your readers' questions. An accurate vocabulary is an essential ingredient of good writing.

It's so essential, in fact, that I'm going to write a whole chapter on it later in the book. In the meantime, I want you to be expanding your own. Thus . . .

VOCABULARY EXERCISE #1

Find a word a day for the next seven days. Don't look for words to impress people with, though. And don't select words you won't feel confident using. Instead, find words you *can use*, in conversation and writing.

There are at least three ways you can go about finding these words. (1) Pick words out of something you're reading . . . words you don't normally use but easily could because they clarify something you think, talk or write about. (2) Look in a thesaurus for synonyms of words you tend to repeat too often. Again, though, pick words you're familiar enough with that you can easily begin using them. (3) Thumb through your dictionary.

When you've found a promising word, write it down. Then write out the full definition, including what part of speech it is. And when you're certain you know how to use it accurately—whatever you do, don't guess—use it in an imaginative sentence.

Remember: Pick only words you're likely to use in normal conversation and writing. And do a word a day, rather than several at a time. (You'll be more likely to remember and use them.)

Sample

Word   prudent

Definition   adj. 1. capable of exercising judgment in practical matters, esp. as concerns one's own interests 2. cautious or discreet in conduct; circumspect; not rash 3. managing carefully and with economy

Sentence   Given the degree of his anger, I decided the prudent thing to do was keep my mouth shut.

❦   ❦   ❦

Tip #1

Lots of students have told me they actually enjoy writing when they know no one else is going to read what they've written, but they just can't write for an audience. Some level of that insecurity manifests itself in everyone who is forced or who chooses to write. Writing is a risk situation. But isn't it risk situations (rather than safe ones) that make life interesting? And isn't it by achieving some measure of success in them that we acquire maturity and wisdom? "Sometimes you just have to stand naked" (*from* "It's Alright, Ma . . . I'm Only Bleeding" by Bob Dylan).

It's a lot easier to stand naked
when you don't think anyone's looking.

Beth Chilton Lindsey

CHAPTER 1   ON THE ROAD

CHAPTER 2

i just can't get
into writing

I was sitting in a tent, listening to the rain rattle softly on the canvas. I would rather have been stumbling around in the woods, but since I was confined to the tent I decided to try to devise some solutions to an old problem: how to help students who claim that they can't get into writing.

By the time the sun returned, I had settled on a four-part solution: (1) automatic writing; (2) journal writing; (3) nonimitative writing; and (4) scheduled writing.

THE PROBLEM

Now, I realize that many people who say "I just can't get into writing" mean, quite frankly, that they have no interest in writing . . . they don't give a hoot about it. The reason I'm going to ignore such people in this chapter is not because of snobbery or disdain but because I figure nobody with that attitude would be reading this book. It seems to me that people reading this book who say "I just can't get into writing" mean either that they want to write or that they wouldn't mind writing but, for one reason or another, they can't do it to their satisfaction.

In ninety-nine cases out of a hundred, the main reason people aren't able to write as well as they'd like is simply that they haven't written much. In addition, they've had so little writing instruction, or they've paid so little heed to the instruction they have had, that they don't have a clear

27

perspective on how to write. As a result, writing for them is an awkward and uncertain experience. Generally, all most people need is guidance, practice and a few successful writing experiences to make writing a more comfortable activity.

A NATURAL HIGH

One interesting and beneficial type of writing practice is automatic writing. It's automatic in that, when it's working right, you're not thinking about what you're writing. All you do is write as fast as you can for a predetermined length of time, say, ten minutes. What do you write about? Whatever happens to pass through your mind. Here, I'll show you. (Read as fast as you can.)

Get ready. Clear your mind. Music's on. Will this work on the typewriter? Let's find out. Get ready . . . get set . . . clear mind . . . clear mind . . . go. What do you mean "go"? I've already started. What am I thinking? I'm not thinking. Now what? The music is lush. Lush. Soft. I like it. What am I talking about? This is silly. Garbage. I am controlling the speed of my thoughts. I am thinking just a little faster than I can type. Try not to think about typing and spelling. It's getting in the way. Just open mind and record thoughts. Whatever comes out. Meditation. This is sort of like meditation. Release of stress. Open the channels and let the junk out. Let it out. Come on. Out. Stuck. Stuck. Now what? There's the music again. Like in meditation. The mantra fades in and out. In and out. I think I'm going to start meditating again. I like doing it. But it's too much trouble to do it twenty minutes twice a day. I'm thinking each letter as I type it. This is interfering. It's not automatic enough. It's mechanical. It's bound to interfere. But I'm not always thinking the letters. Or am I? Well, I'm going to watch my mind and see if I do or not. We'll see. There's the music again. I'm still thinking about typing the letters. Maybe that's like the music and the mantra. In and out . . . in and out. Is that the way of all thought? Do all thoughts spiral in and out and up in one's consciousness? How many thoughts do I balance at one time? I must have four going now, at least. It's really probably some incredible number, with new thoughts slipping in one or a few at a time and old ones slipping out. I wonder what my capacity is. How many can I balance at one time? Sometimes I seem to have none. Is that what meditation works toward? No thoughts? No stress, therefore no thoughts? Hmm. There's the music again. Hey, I wasn't thinking about typing. Is that because my brain is juggling to capacity already and something had to get out for a while? Or is only one thought going through the scanner at a time, with the others on other horses on this merry-go-round? Now the music sounds like a merry-go-round. Mozart piano concertos. Good writing music. Many moods, but all subtle. Have I gone crazy? How am I supposed to know? Somebody, please tell me. No. Wait. I don't want to know. I enjoy this illusion of sanity.

SOMETIMES YOU JUST HAVE TO STAND NAKED

You'd think something of more value would pass through a mind in ten minutes. I was too conscious of what I was doing, though, especially for the first few minutes. But it gives you a general idea.

I had hoped I'd do some truly automatic writing to give you an idea of the potential of this exercise. When it's working right—that is, when you reach a point at which you're not conscious of *what* you're writing . . . or even *that* you're writing—you'll lose contact with your conscious reality. Your mind will float downward until ideas, images, memories, feelings are pouring directly from your subsconscious onto the paper. The result is almost always interesting, sometimes even startling. The faster you write, and the less distracted you are, the more likely this is to happen. Doing it regularly and for longer than ten minutes will also make it more likely to happen. So will doing it immediately on waking in the morning, when you're closer to your subconscious than at any other time of the day.

But the main reason I recommend automatic writing is because it breaks down barriers to writing. My automatic writing didn't go very deep, but when I was finished I felt more like writing this chapter than I did before. It put me in the mood to write. It forced everything out of my mind that might have interfered, and it helped me regain the feel of talking on paper. Try it before writing a paper sometime and see if it doesn't make writing feel more natural for you.

Here are the rules I follow for automatic writing. (1) Clear your mind. (2) Start suddenly, to catch your mind off guard . . . be sure you don't start with a thought already in mind. (3) Write as fast as you can, then even faster and faster, trying to catch every word, every thought that flashes into your mind . . . the faster you write, the more thoughts you'll have, and if you drive yourself hard enough, long enough, you may go beyond conscious thought to truly automatic writing. (4) If you suddenly find yourself without a thought, don't stop writing . . . keep that pen (or those typewriter keys) moving fast and constantly and write something like "I don't have a thought . . . my mind's blank" until another thought or word floats into your mind. (5) Don't worry about the mechanics . . . spelling, punctuation, grammar . . . don't even wonder whether you're making any sense . . . just copy down whatever comes through. (I added punctuation to that automatic writing of mine after I'd finished it . . . so you could make *some* sense of it.)

WRITING EXERCISE _____

Do a ten-minute automatic writing. Then, over the next few days, do several more, experimenting with different time limits, different times of the day, different circumstances. And with each one, write faster than on the one before.

A STEP FURTHER

Journal writing takes you a step further toward public writing than automatic writing does because when you write in your journal you do it for an audience (yourself) and therefore you attempt to make sense. At the same time, though, because you know your audience is yourself, you feel free to say what you want to say, the way you want to say it. Thus journal writing helps break down your inhibitions about talking on paper, and it therefore makes you more confident of your ability to write effectively. Though writing for an audience other than yourself can never be this comfortable, writing regularly in your journal will make it easier for you to be more yourself when you do write to be read.

Stay with your journal; like a true friend it will both listen to you and help you grow.

ZEN AND THE ART OF NONIMITATIVE WRITING

I read a novel a few years ago called *Zen and the Art of Motorcycle Maintenance* by Robert Pirsig. The main character was a college writing teacher. I enjoyed reading what he had to say because his perspective and mine were similar. At one point, he clearly articulated a theory I'd been developing about why some people "can't" write. Here is part of what he had to say.

from Zen and the Art of
Motorcycle Maintenance
Robert Pirsig

He'd been having trouble with students who had nothing to say. At first he thought it was laziness but later it became apparent that it wasn't. They just couldn't think of anything to say.

One of them, a girl with strong-lensed glasses, wanted to write a five-hundred-word essay about the United States. He was used to the sinking feeling that comes from statements like this, and suggested without disparagement that she narrow it down to just Bozeman.

When the paper came due she didn't have it and was quite upset. She had tried and tried but she just couldn't think of anything to say.

He had already discussed her with her previous instructors and they'd confirmed his impressions of her. She was very serious, disciplined and hard working, but extremely dull. Not a spark of creativity in her anywhere. Her eyes, behind the thick-lensed glasses, were the eyes of a drudge. She wasn't bluffing him, she really couldn't think of anything to say, and was upset by her inability to do as she was told.

SOMETIMES YOU JUST HAVE TO STAND NAKED

It just stumped him. Now *he* couldn't think of anything to say. A silence occurred, and then a peculiar answer: "Narrow it down to the *main street* of Bozeman." It was a stroke of insight.

She nodded dutifully and went out. But just before her next class she came back in *real* distress, tears this time, distress that had obviously been there for a long time. She still couldn't think of anything to say, and couldn't understand why, if she couldn't think of anything about *all* of Bozeman, she should be able to think of something about just one street.

He was furious. "You're not *looking!*" he said. A memory came back of his own dismissal from the University for having *too much* to say. For every fact there is an *infinity* of hypotheses. The more you *look* the more you *see*. She really wasn't looking and yet somehow didn't understand this.

He told her angrily, "Narrow it down to the *front* of *one* building on the main street of Bozeman. The Opera House. Start with the upper left-hand brick."

Her eyes, behind the thick-lensed glasses, opened wide.

She came in the next class with a puzzled look and handed him a five-thousand-word essay on the front of the Opera House on the main street of Bozeman, Montana. "I sat in the hamburger stand across the street," she said, "and started writing about the first brick, and the second brick, and then by the third brick it all started to come and I couldn't stop writing. They thought I was crazy, and they kept kidding me, but here it all is. I don't understand it."

Neither did he, but on long walks through the streets of town he thought about it and concluded she was evidently stopped with the same kind of blockage that had paralyzed him on his first day of teaching. She was blocked because she was trying to repeat, in her writing, things she had already heard, just as on the first day he had tried to repeat things he had already decided to say. She couldn't think of anything to write about Bozeman because she couldn't recall anything she had heard worth repeating. She was strangely unaware that she could look and see freshly for herself, as she wrote, without primary regard for what had been said before. The narrowing down to one brick destroyed the blockage because it was so obvious she *had* to do some original and direct seeing.

He . . . concluded that imitation was a real evil that had to be broken before real rhetoric teaching could begin. This imitation seemed to be an external compulsion. Little children didn't have it. It seemed to come later on, possibly as a result of school itself.

That sounded right, and the more he thought about it the more right it sounded. Schools teach you to imitate. If you don't imitate what the teacher wants you get a bad grade.

        ❦   ❦   ❦

Several years ago I decided to do something about the sameness of the writing the students in my classes had been handing in. Until that time, I had been having them write about issues of current social relevance, such as the war in Vietnam, social injustice, ecology. Since they had done little if any thinking of their own about these issues, what they turned in was inevitably repetition of what they had heard or read.

When I realized further that the approach I was using was merely reinforcing what they had been taught to do all along . . . imitate . . . I began asking for writings about themselves, people they knew, events in their lives . . . topics about which they *had* to be original and about which they should have plenty to say. My, how the writing has improved.

(I don't mean to give imitation a totally bad reputation, though; there are times when it can be helpful. Imitation of other writers' styles can help you develop your own style. And imitation of a formula, such as Beth's story in Chapter 1, can help you develop your sense of form. Such imitation is valuable only for practice and skill development, though. It's a means to an end, not to be confused with the end itself, which is, of course, originality.)

WRITING EXERCISE _____

Write about the little finger on your left hand, unless you're left-handed, in which case write about the little finger on your right hand. Write steadily for an hour, spending as little time as possible thinking and as much as possible writing. If at some point you think you've said all there is to say, look closer, think harder. Besides allowing you to do some original thinking and writing, this exercise will help you develop your natural style. It is also an opportunity for you to employ your imagination and humor, if you're so inclined. Write primarily for yourself but be aware of the possibility that someone else might be interested in reading what you have to say about your little finger.

& & &

Writing about something like your little finger (or the front of a building) . . . like journal writing and automatic writing . . . gives you uninhibited practice at talking on paper. Therefore, it helps develop confidence that you can be yourself and be effective when you write. It also takes you a step further into public writing than journal and automatic writing because there is at least the possibility that it will be read. (It might even turn out to be *worth* reading, though that's not the main emphasis of the exercise.) The public/private nature of this exercise makes it a transition between private writing (journal and automatic) and public writing, like the Suggested Public Writing later in this chapter. (Ah! Something to look forward to.)

MAKING TIME

After doing a few automatic writings, making several lengthy journal entries and writing about your little finger, you should have broken through most of what might be blocking you and started the river of words flowing.

> The sun has just set downriver.
> The water in front of me is wide
> and alive with silver ripples.

The next step is public writing itself, the basic principle for which is the same as for the little-finger exercise: Don't imitate. Don't write what you've heard or read about something. If that's all you have to say, you shouldn't be writing about it. (What of value can you possibily have to say about something you haven't experienced?) Write only about what you know from your own first-hand experience. You'll find the writing both easier and more enjoyable. Your readers will enjoy it more, too; they're interested in what *you* see, think, experience . . . not what you've read or heard others say. I'd much rather read about someone's psychic Aunt Betsy than suffer through that person's unoriginal thoughts on extra-sensory perception. (This principle of nonimitative writing is obviously not true for some kinds of writing, such as reports and research papers. Still, the confidence you develop doing original writing can only improve your ability to write about what you've read when you're asked or told to do so. You'll *know* you can handle the writing; all you'll need to find out is the subject.)

What stops many people at this point is the mistaken notion that they have experienced nothing worth writing about. I say "mistaken" because if you're alive you have plenty that's worth writing about. Your life doesn't have to be full of exciting and unusual experiences; what matters isn't the nature of your experience but the way you look at it, the way you understand what it has taught you, the way you feel about it. What I'm going to do for the rest of this book is help you locate the meaningful experiences in your life and plan ways to write about them that will make them as interesting and meaningful to other people as they are to you.

> "Git on hyar 'n ride," twangs
> a young father to his two-year-
> old son, gesturing toward the
> small aluminum circus elephant
> mounted on a large spring.
>
> The boy climbs on, grabs ahold
> of the metal rods protruding
> from the elephant's ears, and
> rocks wildly.

> His mother smiles proudly
> through missing teeth.

The next principle of effective public writing is that it has to be carefully planned and given enough time. One reason people have trouble with writing is that they write hastily and without much planning, anywhere they happen to be, when they just can't put it off any longer. You'll never produce anything you'll be satisfied with if you go at it haphazardly.

> "C'mon, Baby," calls a tired
> white-haired man. "Psst.
> Psst. C'mon, Baby."
> Leash in hand, he is in
> slow pursuit of a hairy
> Yorkshire terrier
> that is scampering like a
> chipmunk around the park.
>
> Catching ahold of the dog's
> passing tail, the man's
> brown-wigged wife says, "I
> think he's tired out now, Hon."
>
> The man sighs as he hooks the
> leash to the tiny collar.

To give yourself the time you'll need to create effective writings, set up a writing *schedule*. Find six hours (or more) in your normal week which you can designate as your writing time. I recommend two sessions a week, either three hours each or four and two, with the first session for writing and the second for editing and rewriting. Or you can spread your schedule over the whole week, an hour here, an hour or two there . . . whatever you think will work best for you. But whatever schedule you decide upon, *commit* yourself to it. During those same hours each week, do nothing but work on your writing. Let nothing interfere.

Telephone: Ring. Ring. Ring.

Bob: Hello?

Marge: Hi, Bob.

Bob: Marge! How *are* you? Gee, it's good to hear your voice.

Marge: Bob . . . why don't you come over tonight. I feel like partying.

SOMETIMES YOU JUST HAVE TO STAND NAKED

Bob: Gulp. Gosh, Marge, I'd really love to. But you've called in the middle of my writing schedule. I'm sorry, but I've committed myself to write during this time and I can't let anything interfere.

Marge: Yeah? Well, I hope you write a masterpiece, you jerk.

Telephone: CLICK!

> The river is hazing over, but
> the silver ripples continue to
> dance. A speedboat slips
> downriver, leaving a widening
> silver V.

A student came to me a few years ago and said he wanted to become a professional fiction writer. His writing wasn't encouraging, but he was determined. And he was in a hurry; he didn't want to spend years becoming a writer. So I told him to set up a schedule of times during the week when he could write. And I told him that the more time he could give to that schedule the faster his writing would improve. Well, he spent an average of forty hours a week writing. And that didn't include all the time he spent reading other writers and reading about writing. Before the year was over, he was writing stories that were good enough to send to magazines. Now I'm convinced that anyone can become as good a writer as he or she wants; all it takes is motivation . . . and time, *scheduled* time.

> It's dark now. The park is
> nearly deserted. Two barges
> slide downriver ahead of a
> noisy, churning tug.

Ed: Hold it a minute!

Me: Hi, Ed. I figured I'd be hearing from you.

Ed: Well, what did you expect? What's the point of mixing these river park scenes in with a perfectly good explanation of the importance of scheduling time for writing?

Me: It's just an experiment. But if you had to ask, I guess it didn't work.

Ed: An experiment in confusion?

Me: No, juxtaposition. I was down at the river trying to finish this section, and I found everything there so interesting that I wrote about it, too. Then I shuffled it all together to see what would happen. I think it creates some interesting effects.

Ed: But . . .

Me: You have to try out new ideas, Ed, if only to develop a sense of their possibilities.

Ed: You like juxtaposition, huh? Well, here's one: *your* textbook next to a *real* composition textbook.

Me: You're taking this too seriously, Ed. But thanks anyway for the compliment.

& & &

Tip #2

If you're trying to describe a scene, like that one at the river, go there . . . keep your eyes and ears open . . . and take notes on what you see and hear.

If you're trying to explain something that exists in your head (a place you've been, a person you've known, something that's happened to you, a fantasy), recreate it in detail in your mind and take notes on what you see and hear.

If you're trying to describe and explain a person you know now, spend some time observing that person and taking notes on what he or she looks like, says and does.

Turn your notes into a finished draft during the time you've scheduled for writing.

Put it away for a day or two. Then rewrite it . . . polish it . . . make it you.

& & &

Tip #3

In addition to finding enough time for writing, you need to find the right place. It should be a place where you feel comfortable, where all your writing needs are at hand (including dictionary, thesaurus, handbook) and where you'll be undisturbed. Music can also help. Instrumental albums can provide both mood and rhythm. Some people can write with the radio on, but I can't; it changes too much.

I've recently added something new to my writing place. Because I spend so much time writing and typing, and because I hate what sitting for hours does to my body, I had a friend build a stand-up writing and typing table for me. (It worked for Hemingway.) I'm standing at it right now, as a matter of fact. And it just occurred to me that if I removed my clothes now

SOMETIMES YOU JUST HAVE TO STAND NAKED

I'd give the title of this book a new meaning: Sometimes you just have to stand naked. (I think I just embarrassed Ed.)

   ♏ ♏ ♏

VOCABULARY EXERCISE #2

As in the Vocabulary Exercise in Chapter 1, find a word a day for the next seven days. If your vocabulary is weakest in one area, verbs for example, find some words in that area that you can begin using immediately. Define them and use them in sentences that have something to do with your reality.

Sample

Word akimbo

Definition adv. adj. with hands on hips and elbows bent outward

Sentence He tried to disguise his discomfort by standing with his arms akimbo, but he didn't fool her.

   ♏ ♏ ♏

SUGGESTED PUBLIC WRITING #1

This is the first of these; there will be seven all together. They are different from the Writing Exercises you'll find in most chapters, which are designed to help you develop specific skills. These Suggested Public Writings are opportunities for you to use all the skills you possess. They should be written as if for publication in a suitable magazine or newspaper.

  By "suggested" I don't mean that you have the option to write or not to write. You have to write something; it just doesn't have to be what I've suggested. The purpose of the suggestion is to stimulate something that may be worth writing about, if you don't already have something you'd rather write.

  Okay, here's your first suggestion. Earlier you wrote a profile of someone you'd just met. Now I'd like you to profile someone you *do* know . . . not necessarily someone you love or even like; just someone you know well. (You might want to look into your past, especially if you can't think of anyone suitable in your present.) The only other guideline to follow in selecting the person you'll write about is that the person be somehow interesting . . . interesting generally, or interesting for something in particular, such as a sense of humor, an eccentricity, a special skill . . . something that he or she is or has done.

Audience. You'll be writing this for a magazine (or newspaper) whose readers are interested in whatever it is that you find interesting about this person. For example, the readers of a women's magazine would be interested in reading about someone who had done and/or said something unusual that has to do with being a woman. Readers of a religious publication would be interested in reading about someone who is somehow inspiring. If your subject appeals to a more general audience, write for a general-interest magazine.

Purpose. There could be several. Generally, your purpose in this writing is to help your readers appreciate this person as much as you do. To do this, you'll have to use details to show what's interesting about the person; generalizations won't do the job. Other purposes could be to entertain the readers, to warn them about such people, to turn them on to such people, to teach them something, to make them feel a certain way, etc. There might be a specific point you would want to make (preferably without stating it), such as "Some of the most interesting people are ones most people have never heard of" or "Some people are worth spending time with because they make life interesting (or exciting)."

Length. Whatever it takes to do it right.

& & &

Ed: Excuse me.

Me: Yeah, Ed?

Ed: Do you mind if I make a suggestion?

Me: Not at all. The more the better.

Ed: Thanks.

ED'S ALTERNATE FOR SUGGESTED PUBLIC WRITING #1

In rhetorical terms, what "Me" is suggesting (in his usual indirect way) is that you *define* something using *examples.* While he suggests focusing on a particular person and implying what it is that he or she represents for you, I would like to suggest a more direct approach. Write an essay in which you explain what certain people are like, using someone you know as an example. Or, if you know several people you could use as examples, give several examples. Sample thesis: Some boys/men just don't know how to behave on a date. Or: The most devout people are usually the ones who don't make a show of their devotion. Or: The people I love the most are the ones who need me the most. Or: Avoid people who only talk about what's on television. In other words, use one or more examples to define a type of person or behavior.

What follows is what one student wrote . . . using my suggestion, not Ed's. I'm including it only because it's an effective writing, and definitely not to suggest that you should write something similar. If you can write humorously or about someone humorous, for example, please do; there's little enough humor in this world. Or, if you like Ed's suggestion, then use it.

Charlie
Glenn Tanner

Charlie Tanner spends most of his time these days sitting on the rickety side porch of his crouching old white-shingled house out on Harmon's Ferry Road, smoking cigarettes, swatting flies, whistling.

Old age and all the things that come with it have taken their merciless toll of him, but he'll carry on a lively conversation with you, or scuffle with you, until he gets tired of either one and ambles away in search of his rocking chair.

He still has a sharp and relentless memory and a good sense of humor. Once he handed me a piece of paper that had been lying on his smoking stand, a carefully snipped-out photo of Richard Nixon. He looked at me with a smile and a twinkle in his eyes and told me, "Here's the one feller that's lonesomer'n I am."

He has a right to feel lonesome, I suppose, even though his wife of fifty-seven years is still with him. She's a beautiful old lady in her own way, but she gives Charlie a hard time, always moaning and groaning and complaining and worrying about when she's going to die and what will become of "poor old Charlie" when she's gone. I sometimes get the impression from him that he never really liked what she had to say too much to begin with, and all those years together haven't changed it.

My folks used to tell me that he was hard-of-hearing, but I know better because I've been hunting with him. He could hear a squirrel cutting a nut long before I could, or distinguish the sound of one moving through the tree tops from a bird or anything else that might be there. He does fail to hear his wife's complaints and orders sometimes, or something that one of his sons or daughters-in-law says to him. They're always trying to humor him or talk to him like he's a child, and it doesn't interest him, so he doesn't hear them. He's not hard-of-hearing; he just hears what he thinks is worth listening to.

Charlie used to play the fiddle and was really good at it at one time. He played that scratchy old country kind of fiddle, old tunes like "Turkey in the Straw" or "Redwings." He'll play every once in a while now, if you can talk him into it. He'll make excuses, "Ain't got no rosum fer my bow," or sometimes complain about his arthritis. But after some coaxing he'll go out to the hall dresser and pull his old red fiddle out of its hiding place, put on his glasses and sit down in his rocker. The first thing you know, he's patting his foot on the floor and squawking out those old tunes about as good as ever.

He was one hell of a man in his day, six feet tall, lanky, with long sinewy arms wrapped in bulging veins. His hands were lean and fairly large and he had the strongest grip of any man I ever knew. He was a carpenter by trade, specializing in barn construction, so he worked with heavy tools and materials that kept his body trim and powerful. He looked as though he was made of tightly strung steel wire, and the look in his eyes, his wit, and his body language let it be known that there were a lot of volts running through those wires. He still has quite a grip in those hands.

Charlie doesn't farm anymore, but when he did his crops were the kind that the neighbors took notice of. He never owned or used a tractor in his life; the old-time way with a team of horses was his method until he retired. He likes to brag about some of his horses, how well they worked with him, like plowing tobacco with Old Nell: "I could just throw the lines over my shoulder'n she'd go right on; I'd say 'gee' or 'haw' at the ends of the rows and she'd go right on, pretty as ye please, and never step on a plant."

His hands are moving constantly as he tells his stories, pointing, waving, acting out every word. "Old Dude was the best bird dog I ever had; he'd run squirrels too. I'd hear him a-runnin' one over yonder in them woods," he'd say, pointing across the yard in front of the house, "then I'd hear 'im let out a-barkin' and perty soon he'd come up in the yard with a squirrel in his mouth that he'd caught on the ground." With that, he'd make a sweeping motion in front of him and snap his fist shut and wink, and inevitably add, smiling, "I turned down a hunnert dollars fer him one time."

Repeating old stories and cracking jokes occasionally or playing tricks are about all Charlie does anymore. To some it may seem senile and childish, but to all who love him it's meaningful and beautiful. I've sat many hours listening to him tell all those tales, even the ones I'd come to know almost by heart, spellbound and unaware of anything else going on around us.

Charlie will probably never chop another boar possum out of a log, or swim in Rough Creek, or hunt the woods with a bird dog again. An almost fatal stroke ten years ago ended that life for him. But while crippling his body, it only slightly ebbed the love of life within him. His spirit is still there, and it shows itself often, sparkling through his filmy tired eyes when he spins a yarn . . . reliving all the happier days . . . rocking . . . whistling.

SOMETIMES YOU JUST HAVE TO STAND NAKED

Survival isn't important.
What matters is *how* you survive.

Tom Robbins
Even Cowgirls Get the Blues

CHAPTER 3

Be yourself

I have spent the last half hour preparing to write. I began by tucking in the kids, then I cruised about the upstairs, loading the washer and dryer, putting away shoes, books, stuffed animals, records, flushing the toilet . . . then downstairs, straightening the kitchen, hanging up towels, turning off lights, feeding the cat and dog, chasing the neighbor dog away from their food, "Git home, you glutton" . . . locking the door . . . then finally into my writing place . . . clearing the desk of grade-school spellers, half-finished drawings, junk mail . . . arranging typewriter, pens, pencils, stencils, dictionary, thesaurus, handbook, razor blade (in case I become suicidally discouraged) . . . back to the kitchen for a beer . . . hey, peanuts! . . . then back to the study, placing beer and nuts in a convenient spot, looking through records for the "right" music for this chapter, flip, flip, nope, flip . . . ah, Fogelberg and Weisberg . . . put it on, sit in rocker, light cigarette, pick up record jacket to write on, cross left leg over right leg, secure paper to record jacket with thumb of left hand . . . Fogelberg staring at me . . . drag on cigarette, eat a few nuts, sip beer . . . put pen against paper . . . begin writing . . . all this time thinking *intensely* about what to say and how to say it, rethinking a week of ideas and plans, putting myself more and more in the mood, until I'm finally committed to writing tonight.

Some people think such behavior strange. I don't. I go through something resembling that process whenever I need or want to write anything important. I become a compulsive straightener, an order freak. Once I have everything in its place, once I have my external environment in

43

order (and therefore apparently under control), I'm ready to order my internal environment, my thoughts. (Doing a quick writing like the one with which I opened this chapter helps, too . . . or, as I suggested earlier, an automatic writing.)

What do *you* do to prepare yourself to write? If you don't already have some mindless, mechanical ritual, one that frees your mind for about a half hour of intense and focused thinking, you ought to develop one. It helps.

Enough on that. Here comes someone interesting.

EVEN COWGIRLS GET THE BLUES

Sissy Hankshaw, the main character in *Even Cowgirls Get the Blues*, is born with unusual thumbs. By the time she's eighteen, they're the size of large cucumbers.

Does she walk around with her hands in her pockets? Does she join a carnival freak show? Does she become a cloistered nun? Does she think of herself as handicapped? No. . . . She becomes a hitchhiker!

from Even Cowgirls Get the Blues
Tom Robbins

From Whitman to Steinbeck to Kerouac, and beyond to the restless broods of the seventies, the American road has represented choice, escape, opportunity, a way to somewhere else. However illusionary, the road was freedom, and the freest way to ride the road was hitchhiking. By the seventies, so many young Americans were on the road that hitchhiking did take on . . . characteristics of sport. In the letters column of pop culture magazines such as *Rolling Stone,* hitchhikers boasted of records set for speed and distance, and whole manuals were published to advise those new to the "game."

Oddly enough, Sissy was almost indifferent to this cultural phenomenon. To approach her for practical advice on the subject of hitchhiking would have been virtually futile. For example, she could not have told you, as did Ben Lobo and Sara Links in their booklet *Side of the Road: A Hitchhiker's Guide to the United States,* that Montana laws strictly forbid hitchhiking in the vicinity of mental institutions. And it is difficult to say how she might have reacted to this piece of advice in *Hitchhikers' Handbook* by Tom Grimm: "Don't use your thumb to hitchhike. Use a sign instead."

And at *this* Grimm observation, "I doubt whether most girls could safely hitchhike long distances alone," Sissy would have had to laugh.

Because by that day . . . Sissy could say:

"Please don't think me immodest, but I'm really the best. When my hands are in shape and my timing is right, I'm the best there is, ever was or will be.

SOMETIMES YOU JUST HAVE TO STAND NAKED

"When I was younger . . . I hitchhiked one hundred and twenty-seven hours without stopping, without food or sleep, crossed the continent twice in six days, cooled my thumbs in both oceans and caught rides after midnight on unlighted highways, such was my skill, persuasion, rhythm. I set records and immediately cracked them; went farther, faster than any hitchhiker before or since. As I developed, however, I grew more concerned with subtleties and nuances of style. Time in terms of m.p.h. no longer interested me. I began to hitchhike in something akin to geological time: slow, ancient, vast. Daylight, I would sleep in ditches and under bushes, crawling out in the afternoon like the first fish crawling from the sea, stopping car after car and often as not refusing their lift, riding only a mile and starting over again. I removed the freeway from its temporal context. Overpasses, cloverleafs, exit ramps took on the personality of Mayan ruins for me. Without destination, without cessation, my run was often silent and empty; there were no increments, no arbitrary graduations reducing time to functional units. I abstracted and purified. Then I began to juxtapose slow, extended runs with short, furiously fast ones—until I could compose melodies, concerti, entire symphonies of hitch. When poor Jack Kerouac heard about this, he got drunk for a week. I added dimensions to hitchhiking that others could not even understand. In the Age of the Automobile—and nothing has shaped our culture like the motor car—there have been many great drivers but only one great passenger. I have hitched and hiked over every state and half the nations, through blizzards and under rainbows, in deserts and in cities, backwards and side-ways, upstairs, down-stairs and in my lady's chamber. There is no road that did not expect me. Fields of daisies bowed and gas pumps gurgled when I passed by. Every moo cow dipped toward me her full udder. With me, something different and deep, in bright focus and pointing the way, arrived in the practice of hitchhiking, I am its cortex and its medulla, I am its foundation and its culmination, I am the jewel in its lotus. And when I am really moving, stopping car after car, moving so freely, so clearly, so delicately that even the sex maniacs and the cops can only blink and let me pass, then I embody the rhythms of the universe, I feel what it is like to *be* the universe, I am in a state of grace.

"You may claim that I've an unfair advantage, but no more so than Nijinski, whose reputation as history's most incomparable dancer is untainted by the fact that his feet were abnormal, having the bone structure of bird feet. Nature built Nijinski to dance, me to direct traffic. And speaking of birds, they say birds are stupid, but I once taught a parakeet to hitchhike. Couldn't speak a word, but he was a hitchhiking fool. I let him get rides for us all across the West, and then he indicated that he wanted to set out on his own. I let him go and the very first car he stopped was carrying two Siamese cats. Tsk. Tsk. Maybe birds are stupid at that."

❀   ❀   ❀

Ah, Sissy. In spite of enormous pressure to the contrary, she was determined to be herself, whatever that might turn out to be. What an interesting world this would be if we all had that attitude. Instead, most people seem determined to conform . . . to hide their differences rather than celebrate them.

CHAPTER 3   BE YOURSELF

That's even true in writing. And it's one reason why so many people have so much difficulty with writing. They're not being themselves. So, naturally, writing is uncomfortable for them. Like Robert Pirsig, I think the main cause of this is the school system, which, when it bothers at all to teach students how to write, forces them to conform to a standard style. The result is that most of what the typical student writes could have been written by any one of millions of other students. Most student writings are not only undistinguished, they're indistinguishable. And boring.

Though you may be comfortable with your writing style because it's *not* different, think about this: If it's not as different as you are, it's not going to be interesting to read.

WRITING EXERCISE _____

(1) Setting: quiet room, candlelight, incense, unobstrusive music. (2) Clear your head. Relax. Don't think about anything. (3) When you and your mind are settled, let thoughts begin again . . . and listen to the voice of your thoughts. (4) When you hear the voice, copy down exactly what it says . . . exactly . . . word for word the way it says it. Don't worry if it jumps around or refuses to make sense. Just let your mind wander where it will, and let the voice in your mind say anything it wants. (5) Think and write steadily but not as hurriedly as automatic writing. (6) Do this for an hour.

If this exercise works for you, you will write in what is your natural style. It's the style you use when you talk to yourself . . . when you're not trying to impress anybody.

THUMBS UP FOR STYLE

Your writing style is simply the way you talk on paper . . . the words you use, the images, the figures of speech, the sentence structure, the rhythm. It is both a result and a reflection of your experience, your interests, energy, attitudes, humor, your feelings about yourself and others, your life philosophy.

There are three steps in the development of your writing style. The first is simply to *find* it. Most of the writing you've done so far . . . your journal, automatic writing, your pinky profile and, of course, the exercise I just prescribed . . . was at least partly intended to help you uncover your natural style . . . the voice you're most comfortable using.

Once you've found your natural style, the next step is to analyze it to find out what's effective about it. This is what I found when I analyzed mine a few years ago: "It sounds like me and feels comfortable; the vocabu-

SOMETIMES YOU JUST HAVE TO STAND NAKED

lary is fairly well developed; the sentence structure is varied; the punctuation is usually correct. . . ."

After you've patted your style on the back for a while, you're ready for step three: Analyze it again to see how you can make it *more* effective. Identify any flaws or weaknesses, such as limited vocabulary, wordiness, erratic punctuation, monotonous sentence structure, uncertain paragraphing, misspelling, etc. When you've found your most obvious weaknesses, pick one, figure out how to correct it and give yourself a deadline for correcting it. Then do it again with another, and another, and another. . . . (If you know your style has weaknesses but are at first unable to identify them, ask someone else to point them out. Writing teachers are good at that.)

Besides correcting the faults, also be looking for ways to make your style leaner, more precise, more flexible, more colorful. Some ways to do this include developing a more precise vocabulary, learning to use original figures of speech, controlling sentence structure. (See rest of book.)

Whether you're talking about writing, tennis or hitchhiking, the principle is the same: When you improve your style, you increase your effectiveness.

BANG, BANG

Generally, the more unusual a style, the more interesting it is. A person with a unique style (like Tom Robbins) can write about anything and make it interesting. The way he looks at something, the kind of things he says about it and the way he says those things . . . his style, in other words . . . because they're unusual, are interesting.

Most of us come from fairly similar backgrounds and speak fairly standard English. Thus our natural writing styles are fairly standard. They don't have to be, though. The more you get into yourself and your own life rhythms, your quirks and foibles, the more you will probably find both your life-style and your writing style becoming increasingly unique.

An unusual writing style is not an obsolute requirement for interesting writing, though. The writer also has subject and structure to work with. If your style is natural for you, if it's clear and accurate and if you're confident using it, but it's not particularly distinctive, the things you write about and the forms you present them in can be enough to make your writing interesting.

Once you've found your natural writing style, repaired its flaws, begun developing it . . . and become comfortable with it . . . you won't be afraid to write for anyone, not even the strictest teacher. And you'll be able to adapt it to any writing situation, from the least to the most formal.

So, be yourself when you write. Don't try to impress your reader, don't try to imitate anyone else and, above all, don't try to be invisible. If there's no personality in your writing, it's dead. If it's not *your* personality, you're dead. Bang, bang.

⅋   ⅋   ⅋

EXERCISE

The two writings that follow are by students. As you read them, be conscious of the personality of each writer as it shows in his or her vocabulary, figurative language, rhythm, humor and overall attitude toward himself or herself.

This first piece began as one of several different journal entries that Billy has since rewritten and is planning to combine with others to produce a story.

The Goodwill Store
Billy Ellis

Not long ago I visited the Goodwill store. It is a quaint little shop on Saint Ann Street. I go there so that I can buy old and stylish things for cheap money. The cheap old things that I buy there make me feel foxy suave. When I visited the Goodwill store the last time I decided that I would purchase a raincoat. The raincoat that I tried on covered me from the nape of my neck to my ankles. An elderly woman came over to look at me as I was trying it on. She looked at me for a while. I assumed she was a salesclerk. When she smiled I could see deep black ridges between her teeth. The ridges were like the cracks in the earth's eternal multicolored rocks. They led me to picture her in her home on a Sunday night reading a Christian book under a lamp that had a yellow shade on it.

"Fits real well," she said.

I casually mentioned that it did but that I wished it was a little cheaper. (The price tag in its collar said the raincoat cost seven dollars and thirty-five cents.) The woman looked at me puzzled for a moment and then drew out of the raincoat sleeve a white price tag that said it was only a dollar.

"See there," she said, "it's only a dollar. Can't find too many raincoats these days for only a dollar." Her smile was ancient.

I thought the occurrence a little peculiar but was nonetheless pleased to find the object of my fancy reduced to the price of a dollar.

"Well, I guess I'll take it then." My voice was growing louder. When I went to pay the lady at the cash register, the elderly lady walked with me. But when we arrived at the payment spot I began to sense that she was not a clerk but another customer.

"Thanks for the bargain, Elma Lou," she said with a widening smile of antiquity. "See y'all later."

SOMETIMES YOU JUST HAVE TO STAND NAKED

I felt a bit remiss for having mistaken the kind lady for a salesclerk, and as she was leaving I bid her a polite good-bye. Her eyes did not lose the gleam they possessed when she had first set them upon me.

"That'll be seven dollars and thirty-five cents," said the lady at the cash register.

I paid the money and exited as if I was never confused about the price of the raincoat. There was a long vertical mirror on the exterior of the store. I looked into it. For a moment I thought I saw just how much I was.

❀   ❀   ❀

This next piece also began as a journal entry. Janetta later revised it to make it meaningful for others as well as herself.

The Great Apple Heart
Janetta Wilson

In those days, our year began in the heat of fall, when the sun was reluctantly moving back from summer's rule. Lockers came rattling to life in the school's musty halls, basketballs bounced off experienced hands, and the chant of our school song floated up to the open windows. Our marching band was reborn. The season sang of bright sweaters and battered marked books: "Time Will Pass, But Will I" . . . "Teen Rebels." At lunchtime, the line was endless as we banged our trays against the counter, eagerly awaiting the Frisco Stew.

It was the season for cider, and plump juicy apples blushed red from feeling so fat. And sometimes we drove with the headlights off up the road to someone's orchard. There the brave ones scrambled over the sharp black points of the fence and shook some stubborn tree until it rained down all the fruit we could carry, extra sweet for being forbidden.

That was the year we were juniors, sullen and ripe and sixteen and ready to burst, either from love or the lack of it. We carried in our purses the brand new driver's license, certificate of our freedom. Last year's boyfriend was cast aside, for the season demanded a bright new star, someone to match the lyrics of the songs: "I Wanna Hold Your Hand" . . . "I'm Leaving It All Up to You."

But then one night I saw one, and never had I seen one like him before. Tall and slender, he had the distinctive air of an older man, with a sparkle of blue eyes that tried to be serious but laughed instead.

We spent that fall sitting at ball games, laughing and teasing with double date couples. The touch of shoulders made everything stop and each of us had to concentrate, staring at the stars until they finally went awash in our gaze. Sometimes a hand would seek a hand and be locked; some nights we held tight in the seat of his humming car, our faces lighted by the pale golden apple of the watching moon. At last we would stand for a few moments, how long you can't measure on clocks, at the front door of my house under the porch light, and the only thing that broke us apart was a wonderful fear, or the sound of my dad clearing his throat.

Cider ran, apples fell and the season burned away. In Dad's car, with Shelta, Sue and Ruth, I sometimes sped past golden fields so fast that they melted together. We cheered because we thought we had outrun everything, the day, the season, the year and all years, and that we would never be caught by them, never pulled anywhere beyond this sixteenth sweet and sour autumn, cussing and kissing as if we had invented them both.

Don't ask me how or why it happened that one November afternoon he lay on the couch in my folks' living room, and insisted on looking ahead. Not to the next day, or week, or year, but just AHEAD, that long unknown shadow. He had to trouble my eyes with the question, "Will you love me then?"

And I didn't ask when, knowing that it was unnameable, but only said softly, "How can we know?"

Not knowing where to stop, he then said, "Well, will you remember this moment, then?"

I crossed my legs underneath me, deep in thought, and hunched over them. Even though the window was letting in a warm flood of light, I shivered.

That night the first snow fell. Cider stiffened and ran no more. The hard joints of the season cracked until the great apple heart could beat no more, except in my mind, where it beats back this song a million years later, and laughs for love.

      🏵   🏵   🏵

What differences did you notice between Billy's style and Janetta's? How do their vocabularies differ? Their figures of speech? Their sentence structures? Their rhythm? Humor? Tone?

How does your own style differ from either of theirs? What have you learned from your analysis of their styles that you can use to make your own more effective?

STYLE SELF-ANALYSIS #1

Identify one strength of your style. Then identify one persistent flaw, decide how to correct it, and set a deadline for correcting it. (Give yourself enough time but no more than you need.) Then determine something else you can do to make your style more effective.

Analyzing your own style like this actively involves you in improving it. When someone else tells you (a teacher, for example), you're only passively involved . . . and less likely to do much about it.

Sample

Strength   I'm careful to use accurate verbs.

Weakness   I sometimes use confusing sentence fragments.

Corrective   Study rules and examples in handbook. If necessary, seek help from tutor and/or teacher.

Deadline   One week from today.

Something else I intend to do to make my style more effective   Try to use similes and metaphors when appropriate.

ANOTHER SIDE OF BEING YOURSELF

When you're confronted with a writing problem, anything from a word choice to an ending, you can take the easy and ineffective option, which is to solve it the way it's already been solved by someone else. Or you can do what you know you should do, which is to solve it in a way that gives your subject, your audience and yourself the credit they deserve. All you need to do is think a little harder than normal.

Say you're trying to describe the way you felt the first time someone looked in your eyes and said, "I love you." You *could* write "I felt like I was on cloud nine" or "I felt the earth move under my feet" or any of dozens of other ways that other people have described such feelings. Or, you could concentrate on the feeling until you figure out what it was like for *you.*

Your feelings, sensations, perceptions and experiences are *unique.* Why deny it by describing them in terms of someone else's experience? Be yourself.

ஃ   ஃ   ஃ

Tip #4

There are three steps to effective writing: planning . . . writing . . . rewriting. Many of the problems people have with writing result from trying to perform all three steps at once. It's frustrating and next to impossible to write well without doing it a step at a time. Try this:

(1) At least a few days before beginning to write, start thinking about what you're going to write. After you've thought of a good subject (one you know enough about that you can explain and show it clearly; one that you care about enough to want to make it perfect), start thinking about the best audience for it, the details you'll need to make it as clear to your readers as it is to you, the most effective way to arrange those details, etc. As ideas occur, write them down. You don't need to set aside special times for doing this; do it during whatever free thinking time you have (driving around, eating, taking a bath, sitting in an uninteresting class, etc.). As a final step, put yourself through an intense thinking session, like the one I described at the beginning of this chapter.

(2) Write when you're supposed to . . . during your scheduled writing time.

(3) When you think the piece is finished, put it away for at least twenty-four hours. It's always difficult to be objective about your own writing, but it's especially difficult right after you've written it. After at least twenty-four hours, read it over critically, making notes for changes. Some parts may need to be reworded, some cut, some moved. Something may even need to be added. When you're satisfied with your content, work on your style until it's as clear and accurate as you can make it. Then work on the mechanics: grammar, punctuation, spelling.

As a writer, you have three personalities: the planner, the writer and the editor/rewriter. Don't confuse them. Let each do his or her own job with minimal interference from the others.

❀ ❀ ❀

Tip #5

The more time you spend with someone, the more you feel at ease and free to be yourself. It's the same with writing. The more you do it, the more comfortable you are with it . . . and the more you are free to bring all of yourself to it. This is even true when you're working on a particular writing. At first, as you struggle to put your ideas and details in some sensible order, it's almost impossible for the whole you to be involved. In those early stages of a writing, about all of you that's working is your reason. But once you're satisfied that you've said all that needs to be said, in an order that makes sense, you begin to relax and more of yourself comes out to explore what you've been doing. What is likely to happen then is you'll realize that, though the writing says what you wanted to say, it doesn't sound like you. At best, it sounds like the formal, logical, serious you. What's missing is your energy, your emotions, your humor . . . in other words, the rest of you. But now, because you're confident that you've said what you wanted, you're free to let the rest of yourself affect the way you're saying it. A couple of rewrites later, with persistence and luck, the writing will be finished. It will be you . . . all of you.

❀ ❀ ❀

Tip #6

Questions you should ask yourself repeatedly while you're working on a writing and after you think it's finished: If this were someone else's writing, would I read it? Would I find it interesting? Be honest. If the answer is "no," figure out what to do to make it interesting.

❀ ❀ ❀

VOCABULARY EXERCISE #3

Again, find a word a day for seven days . . . words that you can begin using immediately. This time concentrate on words that accurately describe aspects of things you've experienced . . . a color of the sky (azure), the quality of a particular smile (intimidating), a feeling (exhilaration) . . . whatever. Then define each word and use it in a sentence pertaining to your experience.

Sample

Word   culmination

Definition   n. 1. a culminating; reaching of the highest altitude or point 2. the highest point; zenith; climax (culminate—to terminate at the highest point; to bring to a close—usually followed by "in")

Sentence   My efforts to think of a humorous way to use the word "culmination" have culminated in my realization that it's not a humorous word.

Dear Sometimes You Just Have to Stand Naked,

I hope you don't mind the outlandish name I've stuck you with. I know it's cumbersome, but I think you'll find it suitable.

Your pal,

Me

Dear Me,

The name's okay; I'm getting used to it. But you should point out that it's an <u>adaptation</u> of Dylan's original line: "Even the president of the United States sometimes just has to stand naked."

On second thought, I'm not so sure I like being placed in that kind of company.

Yours truly,

S. Y. J. H. T. S. Naked

CHAPTER 4

show and tell

Things That Never Get Said
Sue Jarvis

Mom lived in the country all her life. She was a part of the country as it was a part of her. The scheme of life which she had designed for herself was based on country living, welcoming the recurring seasons, watching the new crops come in and watching her man take care of them.

She always looked younger than her years. Her dark hair, gently touched at the temples with white, promised a color of salt and pepper in the coming years. Her unlined face had the color and freshness of the country air, her lightly lashed blue eyes were soft and glowing, and her smile was one the Mona Lisa would envy.

The house sat on a hill, giving a picturesque view of acres and acres of farmland, the bright green grass separated by fences holding cattle and horses in captivity.

She would sit on the swing on the large L-shaped porch shelling peas or breaking beans, getting ready for the hours of canning necessary to feed her brood of children.

She had fourteen children, all very active and time-consuming, except for Raymond Lee who died at six weeks. The girls had to help with the canning, and the boys worked in the fields, and all had to go blackberry picking to get gallons of blackberries for jams, jellies, and the endless blackberry cobblers cooked in the winter.

Many times we would be sitting on the front porch preparing vegetables when a storm would come up. I never remember being frightened of them. She taught us not to be, but to enjoy the colors of a storm and the sweet, fresh smell of the air afterwards.

Mom had enough love for all of us; she always took time to spend with each of us. In the evenings she would spend hours helping me learn to read, going over words again and again, and making stories come alive—giving me the desire to do it all on my own.

Sunday was the holy day. No work allowed, only resting and socializing. Mom needed Sunday's rest to survive the eighteen-hour weekdays. She began the week by doing the piles on piles of laundry on the back porch. We called it the back porch; actually it was a large enclosed room with a cistern in the center, a wood-burning stove over to the left side, a freezer to the right, and the wringer washing machine in the middle. With all the heating and hauling of water for the washer, the laundry would take about two days. The next day would be spent doing all the ironing required in the pre-permanent press days.

Farm life is hectic. Small problems are always cropping up. There was a litter of pigs whose mother wouldn't nurse them; she was killing them off one by one. Mom told Dad to bring them to the house. They were taken to the back porch; Mom filled baby bottles with milk and we fed them. It was really something, watching them suck and gurgle the bottles like starving babies. While we were gone to school, Mom took care of them, giving them their feedings. She babied and played with those little pigs for weeks. Finally they were healthy enough to be returned to their own home. Then something else would take their place, a dog or cat, anything needing loving care and attention.

She looked forward to the weekends when my married brothers and sisters would come home. Mom would cook one of her fantastic dinners; afterwards the grown-ups would sit around and play cards while the kids played Old Maid, Monopoly, checkers. That is, until "Gunsmoke" came on; then the popcorn would be popped and the lemonade poured, and everyone would gather before the tube to see what kind of bad guys ole Matt Dillon and Chester would catch, and of course they always got their man. After the varmints were caught, the games would start again. Mom would run around waiting on everyone, especially her sons- and daughters-in-law. Every one of them was perfect to her, and they could do no wrong. She would spend as much time doing for them as for her own kids. One of them, Curtis, was crazy about home-churned butter. Mom would spend hours churning butter just for him. Once she spent almost six months hand-stitching a quilt for one of her daughters-in-law who wanted one with a special design.

Mom and Dad were always poor, rarely having enough money for anything other than the bare necessities of life. Of course, that meant that we had hand-me-down clothes. When one outgrew something, the next in line would get it. But there were occasional good years on the farm, years when, if everything went right, there would be a few more dollars than usual.

Once, I don't remember if it was one of the "prosperous" years or not, a neighbor's home burned. Everything was lost except the clothes they were wearing. Mom bought them a set of dishes, and I saw red. I could have had a dress or shoes or something with the money she spent on those dishes. What did it matter to me that they had nothing left, no clothes, no furniture, no dishes . . . nothing.

The one Christmas I will never forget was 1957. Daddy always went to

SOMETIMES YOU JUST HAVE TO STAND NAKED

the grocery on Saturday mornings. Linda, a younger sister, and I would go with him. One Saturday we saw this doll way up high on the shelf. It was about twenty-four inches tall, with blonde hair and painted lips, and it had on a long blue silk and lace dress. It was the most beautiful doll we had ever seen, and, oh, how we wanted it. Every Saturday after that we would stand and look at the doll while the shopping was being done. We knew we could never have it; we were satisfied with just visiting rights.

Christmas finally dawned, a special day for everyone. Apples, bananas, oranges, nuts, Cokes were brought out . . . all the extravagant items that we could not afford during the rest of the year. After a big dinner we all tied into our gifts, and, miracle of miracles, Linda and I got our dream doll. We took turns owning her.

Frankie, an older brother, and the best-looking member of the family, got us a new sweater. A brand new sweater. It just had to be the best Christmas ever. I'm sure we received something else, but the doll and the sweater faded all else out. Frankie was home on Christmas vacation from school. He had a couple of weeks off, and spent most of the time working in town to earn extra money to go with what he earned working summers and after school. Dad was a little upset on this day; he needed money to pay off some cattle and didn't know where he would get it. Frankie took out every penny he had, all his school money, and gave it to Dad, saying, "Here, Pop, take this. I can always earn more." Dad at first didn't take it; then he gazed up at Frankie, looked down and took the money. I guess he realized that love was being given him, something I was far too young and selfish to understand. Frankie then grabbed and lifted me to the ceiling, saying, "Babe, do you like your sweater?"

Those were the last words I ever remember hearing him say. The next night he was lying in a hospital, unconscious from a car accident.

It was hardest on Mom. The love she had for each of us was very special. She spent the next few years taking care of Frankie. The first weeks she spent night and day by his side; then she went to Nashville with him, praying through all the surgeries. She stayed at the hospital with him for months, giving him the around-the-clock attention he needed, seeing new tubes go in him every day and suffering with each one. Still she hung on, taking care of him and praying, always praying for some miracle, a miracle that never came.

Eventually he was brought home. The doctors said there was nothing more that could be done for him, just take care of him. He was still in a hospital bed, still unconscious, and still required around-the-clock attention. We took shifts, Mom staying up with him most of the time, getting her work done when she could. She would spend hours rubbing his hands and patting his face, talking to him, telling him she loved him, and still praying for that miracle.

How she still had time for the rest of us, I don't know, but she always did. Our aches and pains were given individual attention, and she made each of us feel we were special.

Her life soon took on even more worries. Frankie's hospital bills were staggering, as were his monthly drug and doctor bills. They had been paying a set amount to both Nashville and Greenville each month. It was fine with Nashville, but Greenville's administrator suddenly decided he wanted his then and there, and in one lump sum. Of course, it couldn't be paid. He realized that, and offered to buy the farm so the debt could be settled. After hearing an emphatic no, he filed a lawsuit to force the sale of the farm.

During this period, an oil firm came in and began drilling on the farm, fulfilling an old contract. Each day we watched the drilling. It was an interesting sight; however, if they didn't hit soon, we would lose the farm. The court kept giving Dad time, but the final court date was coming up fast. As it drew nearer, the tension increased. Mom still didn't show the strain she must have been under. Each morning was carried on as usual. The cows were milked, the chickens watered, the house cleaned. Then one morning as the chores were being done, we heard the men from the rig start screaming. Everyone rushed to the rig. They had hit it. The oil began rushing up, up, up, hundreds of feet into the sky, then falling down to the earth, hitting the workers, the family. Everyone was running around with oil in his hair, on his clothes, stepping in pools of it. It just kept shooting up higher and higher, no one bothering to plug it for several minutes. We could keep the farm, pay the hospitals, and take good care of Frankie, all because the earth opened up and gave us its liquid. Mom was happy, Daddy delirious, and the administrator livid.

Life settled again into a routine. Mom continued her seemingly endless canning. And she worked her flower gardens that actually seemed to spurt up on their own with just a look from her soft blue eyes.

One summer I wanted to plant my own flower garden. She marked me off a spot and I worked it myself, hers covering the rest of the hillside. I couldn't wait for the colors to start surfacing. She tried to teach me patience, that it would come in time. But, oh, how hard it was for me. I kept waiting and watching, and finally the hillside was ablaze with flowers, every color imaginable all over the hillside. That is, except for about four square feet where a very few sick-looking yellow flowers swayed in the breeze. It was my spot, all right. I still can't grow anything. I don't have Mom's green thumb, nor her courage, gentleness, or the forgiving nature she displayed so often.

She would forgive anyone anything, always making an excuse for him. When a Baptist minister was at the house one day, praying for Frankie, he turned to Mom and said, "You must have committed some awful sin for Frankie to be unconscious. This is a punishment to you and you will go to hell for whatever sin you committed." Why she didn't throw him out of the house, I don't know. Except, as I said, she was a very forgiving person.

Mom would sit up with Frankie at night, usually until about 2:00 A.M. Then Dad would take over. They were strict parents. We had to be home from dates by 11:00. This gave us opportunities to have private moments with her. I would often come home from dates early just to stay up and talk to her. I firmly believe that I didn't suffer some of the normal teenage anxieties as a result of having her at my side any time I needed her.

I never once heard her shout or scream out in anger, or do any of the other irrational things I do. She may have; I just never heard her. The only time I ever saw her truly upset was one Sunday after I had moved to Owensboro and gone home for the day. It was a beautiful warm summer day, flowers were swaying in the breeze, the cattle grazing in the distance. The greenness of the hills had a calming effect on me. The kids were turning the handle on the ice cream freezer. Mom and I went in to get the dishes for the ice cream. She picked them up, stood frozen for a second, then slammed them on the counter saying "No! No!" and went to the bedroom and shut the door.

I was shocked. I had never seen her really angry, or hurt, or whatever emotion that was. I only knew it was deep.

I never did find out what was wrong that day, but I think I know. Very soon after that, her many trips to the hospital for leukemia began. They started out being for a week, then she would be there several weeks, and then home for a while. Then back for more blood transfusions, with frequent threats of pneumonia, and it finally hitting, placing her in an oxygen tent and no visitors for a week, coming out of it, and it hitting again and again. When she would come out of it, she would be given another room. And in we would go with flowers, kisses, and the first thing she would say was, "Are you all right?" And, "Are you eating good?" And most important, "Take good care of Frankie for me." She was in and out of the hospital for years.

I guess everyone has regrets for something in his past. If not regret, then certainly some other appropriate word. Even now, I sometimes scream out to her, saying, "Why didn't you talk to me about it? You shared everything else. Why not this?" Looking back, maybe I should have asked her if she wanted to talk about her fears of dying. Maybe she did talk to someone, but not me. What if she needed me, as so many times I had needed her, and I wasn't there?

She died on my birthday, just as the sun was coming up. She died without ever hearing all the things I wanted to tell her, things I had had twenty-two years to say, and, somehow, never got said.

⚙ ⚙ ⚙

Ahem. Ah-hmm-hm. Clearing the lump from my throat. I'm such a sucker for a sad story. That was a good one, though, wasn't it? The only thing that infringes on my enjoyment of it is that parts of it are rather sentimental, even if it really did happen that way. I like it, though, because Sue gave me enough details that I could clearly see her mother and her influence on Sue. Of course, she was writing about her mother but I find myself more interested in Sue, especially the way she looks at herself compared to her mother, which she symbolized with the contrast between her mother's garden and her own. Good examples, like Sue's mother, can seem impossible to live up to.

Believe it or not, that piece was originally three times as long as what you just read. Sue worked harder editing and rewriting than she did writing. Good for you, Sue.

SEEING IS BELIEVING

Your natural style should be out in the open by now, busily shedding fat and developing muscle. Keep up your efforts. Meanwhile, I'm going to shift the focus to *content* . . . what information to include and how to arrange it so that your subject will be as interesting and meaningful for your readers as it is for you.

Let's consider the information side of content first. Because writing is work, most people are inclined to provide as little information as possible when they write. And the easiest way to do that is to generalize . . . to *tell* rather than *show*.

What's the difference between writing that tells and writing that shows? Often it's the difference between boring writing and interesting writing. When you tell, you skim the surface of the person or experience you're writing about. When you show, you recreate the person or experience.

Let's say you're writing about a person. And your aim is to clarify why you think that person is interesting or important. If you were merely to tell your readers about the person, you would say things like, "He's my best friend; I like him a lot." Or, "We've had lots of good times together." Or, "She's got her head on straight and knows where she's going." Such statements (generalizations) tell the readers what *you* think about the person; they don't let them see that person for themselves. As a result, the readers don't care; they don't understand, so they're not interested.

To *show* this person to your readers, you'd at least have to follow up your generalizations with examples. You should also include some physical details so the readers can see him or her, and quote the person so the readers can hear him or her. Or maybe, instead of working with generalizations and examples, you could recreate a particular incident that shows this person doing what you consider interesting or important.

Basically, what you do when you *show* is appeal to your readers' senses as much as possible. You give them things to see, hear, smell, maybe even taste and feel. And you do this for two reasons: (1) because the quickest and surest way to the readers' minds and emotions is through their senses; and (2) because writing that appeals to the readers' senses is more interesting for them to read. It gives them pictures and sounds, not just thoughts. It's concrete.

In order to help you understand her mother, Sue selected details and examples from throughout their life together. Early in the writing, she shows you what her mother looked like. And she shows you her world: the farm, the swing, the porches. Then she gives you detailed insights into the kind of person her mother was: helping Sue learn to read, feeding the baby pigs, caring for Frankie and on and on. If she had merely told you about her mother, she would have written only a couple of pages. And you wouldn't know her, you wouldn't understand her effect on Sue, and you wouldn't understand Sue's feelings for her. (You wouldn't enjoy reading it, either.)

SOMETIMES YOU JUST HAVE TO STAND NAKED

Find a small common object in your pocket or purse, on the floor, on the ground, anywhere . . . something you won't mind looking at closely for a while . . . and describe it in writing. In the process, do two things: (1) Describe it *generally*. For example, if you're describing a nickel, describe what a nickel looks like as if your readers had never seen one. Give them enough general details that they could draw an accurate picture of a nickel from your description. (2) Describe it *specifically*. Look at your nickel, or whatever you're describing, closely and find its distinguishing characteristics . . . all the things that make it different from any other nickel. If you look closely enough, you'll find more than you need. If you think you've found everything, look again . . . you've missed something. When you're finished, your readers should be able to draw *your* nickel. Or (if they can't draw), they should be able to find your nickel in a pile of nickels with the same date. If you're describing a maple leaf, the readers should be able to find yours in a small pile of maple leaves.

Let your readers know from the start what it is you're describing; don't play guessing games with them.

Do this exercise in steps: (1) Take notes and decide on an approach, (2) write, (3) edit and rewrite.

After you've completed your notes, but before you begin writing, decide what order to present your details in. If you present them haphazardly, your readers will be confused. You could begin at the top of what you're describing and work your way down. Or you could move from bottom to top, from side to side, from outside in or from inside out. You could move from the general to the specific, or from the specific to the general. You could start at one point and work your way around clockwise or counterclockwise. Or you could create your own order.

This exercise should help you train your eye to see the unusual in the usual . . . to go beyond general to specific . . . to look closely enough at everything (people, trees, clouds, turtles) to find what makes it different and, therefore, interesting. And it should help you realize the importance of presenting information in some kind of order.

SHOWING ENOUGH

The primary aim of communication is understanding. This is easy enough to achieve when you're communicating on a simple level. "Close the door" usually means just that. So do "I never want to see your stupid face again" and "You're under arrest."

The more complex the message, though, the greater the likelihood of its being misunderstood. Which means that, if you want to be understood, you not only have to show, you have to show *enough.*

If I wanted you to understand the impact an automobile accident had on me, I'd do more than just generalize about it. I'd recreate what went on inside and outside of me before, during and after the accident . . . not all of it, of course, but enough of the most significant details: the kind of night it was, the mood I was in, my thoughts, why I was there, things I was seeing and hearing. . . . And I wouldn't tell you I was writing about an accident until I arrived at that point in the story; that way it would be nearly as much of a surprise for you as it was for me. Then I would recreate the sound of squealing tires, the pain in my legs, the lights, sirens. . . . In other words, I'd give you enough details for you to feel what it was like to go through that experience.

If I wanted you to understand how much I enjoyed going hunting with my grandpa when I was a kid, I'd recreate some of our hunting experiences so you could see for yourself where we were, what we were doing, and what we were like together. Or I could recreate one particular day of hunting to show the same thing. If I used the latter approach, I could fill in any necessary background information at convenient places in the narrative. If I couldn't recall one specific day that was interesting or eventful enough, I could select incidents from a few different days and combine them as if they *were* one day. That wouldn't exactly be the truth, but it should make for more interesting reading. (For more on the subject of truth in writing, see Chapter 12.)

WRITING EXERCISE

Go outside. Look around until you find a scene which for some reason is interesting to you. It could be a small section of the ground, something viewed through a fence, any interesting slice of all that's in your view. Then recreate the scene in writing, filling in the general picture with clear, interesting details. Make this word picture so distinct that artistically inclined readers could paint it accurately from your description. To accomplish this you'll have to appeal to the readers' senses, particularly sight. Be sure to show, not tell. Don't say things like "I saw a small bird." That's telling. Instead, show the bird: "A small gray bird darted erratically overhead. (I wish I hadn't been looking up.)"

As in the common object exercise, do this in three steps: plan, write, rewrite. Also, see what you can do to make it interesting, though if the scene you're describing is interesting all you should have to do is recreate it in enough clear detail and it will be interesting to the readers, too. And, finally, present your details in some order. One you might consider, in addition to those mentioned in the object exercise, is to begin with the focus close-up on the most interesting detail in the scene, then slowly widen the focus to include the details around it. Better yet, let your scene tell you the best order to present it in.

IN GOOD FORM

So far I've been talking about the information side of content . . . what kind of details and examples to use. The other side of content is *form* . . . the order in which you arrange those examples and details. (Structure, arrangement, approach, order and organization are all more or less synonymous with form.) All writing has form, of course, since all writing begins in one spot and ends in another. But most writing would benefit from more speculation about how to move the readers most effectively from one spot to the other.

You are making decisions about form in the common object exercise and the scene exercise when you choose to describe from the inside out, or from specific to general, or whatever. The general form of Sue Jarvis' story is chronological: she shows you what her mother was like from early in their relationship on through to its end. My approach to the automobile accident was chronological, too . . . beginning to end, in order. I was talking about form in the Grandpa example, too, when I was talking about whether to take the reader along on several different trips or on one particularly memorable one.

The only real "rule" of form is that it be somehow appropriate. You should have some good reason, for example, for deciding to show something chronologically, or reverse-chronologically, inside out, upside down, pyramidally, juxtapositionally, convergently or topsy-turvily. And that reason should be that it is the most effective form for this subject, this purpose, this audience and, of course, this writer.

There are no limits to the number of different forms that can be devised, just as there's no limit to the number of ways a house can be designed. But for writing to be effective, it must have *some* form, whether conventional or original, or the readers will have unnecessary difficulty following what you're explaining or showing. They'll have stopped to think about something else, while you're still writing along thinking they're there beside you listening. (Hey, where've you been?)

❦   ❦   ❦

Tip #7

One important thing to check when you edit and rewrite is paragraphs. Make sure you have enough. The readers need to rest periodically to reflect on what's been said so far. A paragraph break is a signal for them to do so.

Extremely long paragraphs, like extremely long sentences, tend to result in a loss of the readers' attention; they've been given more than they can absorb. (Paragraphing is another aspect of form. So is what I'm going to say in the next Tip. Form covers a lot, from general structure to sentence structure.)

  ₛ ₛ ₛ

Tip #8

Check to see whether details in one sentence or paragraph really belong together. Keep related information together; keep unrelated information separate. "Six feet tall, his hair was brown." That sentence mixes unrelated details. (It also says that his hair was six feet tall. Bad form, there.)

  ₛ ₛ ₛ

Tip #9

Stuck for an opening? Usually, the form you decide to use will suggest the right opening. If it doesn't, try one of these: Open with concrete details of person, place or action; open with a provocative question or generalization. (Not just any question or generalization, though, but one worth being asked or stated . . . unless you want to appear foolish.) Remember, an effective opening provokes interest, not boredom or derision. As with form, the possibilities for effective openings are endless. Glance through collections of stories and essays and notice the many ways other writers have solved the problem of effective openings.

  ₛ ₛ ₛ

Tip #10

Title your public writings. Here are three criteria for a good title, in order of importance: (1) It should stimulate the readers' interest; (2) it should give at least a vague idea of the content of the writing; (3) it should be five words or less.

  ₛ ₛ ₛ

SUGGESTED PUBLIC WRITING #2

Go to a place where you can have an uncluttered view, probably the country, and observe a sunset (or a sunrise or some other major natural phenomenon). Then share the experience in writing.

Show your readers where you are; give them details of your surroundings, things you hear (birds, crickets, wind, traffic), things you see (cows, hills, trees, clouds); and describe each of these so that the readers

    SOMETIMES YOU JUST HAVE TO STAND NAKED

hear and see them the way you did. Describe in detail the changes in the sun, sky and earth as the sun slides nearer the horizon and finally below it. Show how gradually it alters the way everything looks and feels. Describe its effect on you. A sunset (or sunrise) is not just the sun going down (or coming up); it's a total environmental and, when you're watching it, personal experience.

Writing about a sunset, or showing anything in detail, is more than a mere exercise in descriptive writing. It's a means of forcing yourself to see more than you normally see. If you do it often enough, you'll find that much of what's going on around you is no longer passing you by.

Allow yourself a couple of hours just for the observation and note-taking part of this writing. Arrive at your spot a good hour before the sunset and stay for about as long after.

And remember, you're not writing about sunsets in general, but about this one sunset, which is different from any other sunset that's ever been or will be, and which you see differently from anyone else who's observing it.

Purpose. To share the experience, for whatever it's worth to you. Don't explain (tell) how you felt about it, though; let your details and the way you describe them speak for themselves.

Audience. One possibility would be people who already appreciate this sort of thing. Another would be people who are unaware of or apathetic about the value of natural phenomena. After reading what you've written, they should think about what they've been missing and resolve to pay closer attention from now on so that they can enjoy the kind of pleasure they watched you enjoying. Again, though, whatever you do, don't *tell* them that's what they ought to think. There's no faster way to turn off readers than to start preaching to them. (Look who's talking.)

Form. One you might consider would be to put your observations into some context. For example: "I was driving home from school the other evening, irritated with everything. Not wanting to infect everybody at home with my rotten mood, I turned onto an old road, parked the car and began walking. As I rounded a bend in the road, the sun. . . ."

ED'S ALTERNATE

In rhetorical terms, what "Me" is asking you to do this time is describe a *process* (the sun setting) and at the same time show its *effect* on the environment and yourself. Those are useful writing methods: process analysis and cause-effect analysis. But who wants to read about a sunset?

Why not use one or both of those methods for something more relevant? For example, you could use process analysis to explain the steps involved in doing something you know how to do, such as growing vegetables organically, or making someone notice you and finally ask you for a date. And you could use cause-effect analysis to explain what happens when you try to do something before you're ready, such as trying to hustle someone only to find out that you're the one being hustled. Process analysis is useful for writing about anything involving steps or stages, from baking a cake to building an atomic bomb. Cause-effect analysis is useful for writing about anything involving reasons and consequences, from explaining the reasons (causes) for failure in a ball game to explaining the consequences (effects) of any form of overindulgence.

Think about all the valuable things you know how to do, and all the things you know the causes and/or effects of; you'll come up with something.

& & &

VOCABULARY EXERCISE #4

Whenever you write, you encounter vocabulary problems. Either you notice that you're repeating a word too often, or you can't think of the "right" word for something you're trying to describe or explain. You can solve either problem by using both your thesaurus and your dictionary.

In your thesaurus, find the word you're repeating too often. It will give you several alternates. Pick the one you think will work best; then go to your dictionary to make sure it means what you think it means.

To find that elusive "right" word, look up in your thesaurus words that you know are close to the one you're seeking. When you think you've found it, again use your dictionary to make certain.

At the usual rate of a word a day for seven days, use your thesaurus and your dictionary to solve seven of the vocabulary problems you encounter while doing the Public Writing and the Writing Exercises in this chapter. (If you don't have any problems, make some up.) Use the word-definition-sentence format for writing up the results of your seven vocabulary adventures.

GET OUT OF THE WAY

One last thought about showing. When you're writing, your job is to pass the thing you're writing about on to your readers, with as little interference from yourself as possible. If you merely tell, you're putting yourself in the way of the person or experience you're writing about, thus obstructing its passage to the readers. You're asking the readers to look at you rather than at what you're writing about. What you need to do, if you want your readers to be interested and to understand, is give them the thing itself, not your generalizations about it. Show, don't tell.

The only truly magical and poetic exchanges that occur in this life occur between two people.

Tom Robbins
Even Cowgirls Get the Blues

CHAPTER 5

"not a Bad place to die"

A Solitary Bird, Part III

We turned off the highway onto a narrow blacktopped road and drove toward what looked like a small airport. But as we rounded the last bend, I saw that it wasn't a normal airport ... with concrete runways, lights and emergency vehicles. It was a pasture. At one end of it sat three planes, three little, old Cessna 180s that looked like they'd been painted green with a broom. Beside the pasture stood a Quonset building (the office), a small wooden refreshment stand (closed), some sort of a hut on stilts, and an outhouse.

I stood alone beside the parked car for a moment, looking around at all the people in their colorful baggy nylon jump suits. And it was then I realized that, as I've done so often in my life, I was entering a new experience shrouded in ignorance. I knew next to nothing about parachuting. In fact, what I had in mind was jumping out the side door of something like a B-29, as I'd seen all those GIs do in the war movies. It was suddenly clear, though, that the folks at Greene County Sport Parachute Center had something quite different in mind. They were going to teach us to be skydivers ... free-fallers ... daredevils.

When the eight of us were finally all together in the grassy parking area, we walked quietly toward the Quonset building, where we signed in and paid our $31 apiece (for instructions, equipment rental and one jump). Then we were led to a field about 100 yards away, where we were to undergo several hours of instruction.

Our instructor was young, but experienced: "I've been up and down over 300 times." I was impressed. Unfortunately, though, he wasn't much of a teacher. He'd start out telling us something, then say, "Maybe I ought to tell you about that later." Or, "Oh, no, wait; that's not right. Let me go over that again."

He didn't do much for my confidence.

He did make one remark, though, which eased my anxiety enough that I almost began to like him: "Now, just because you paid your $31 doesn't mean you'll get to jump today. I might not think you're ready. Or it might be too windy."

Too windy? Maybe I can get out of this gracefully yet, I thought. Come on, wind.

Then the instructor laid out a parachute and introduced us to its parts: toggles, lines, shroud . . . uh . . . hmm . . . I can't remember any more. Then he explained how to guide it: "Pull on this right toggle and the chute turns to the right. . . ."

After about an hour of that, he led us over to one of the little green airplanes to explain the proper way to enter it. It's not as simple as you might think. These were small, single-engine planes, with only one seat, the pilot's. Yet four more men, wearing boots, jump suit, helmet and two parachutes each, would have to squeeze in there, too.

Each of us began the practice entry by sitting in the doorway, feet hanging down outside the plane. Then we were taught how to maneuver into our special spots in the tiny enclosure. The first one in, the jump master, had to turn and crawl to a kneeling position behind the pilot's seat. The next one had to crawl backwards till he bumped into the rear of the cabin, then scoot over and kneel behind the jump master. The third crawled backwards until he was beside the second. And the last one in turned around and sat next to the pilot, on the floor, facing the rear of the plane. The way we were packed in there reminded me of that old Stan Frieberg tomato paste commercial: Voice #1 . . . "How did they get those eight great tomatoes in that little bitty can?" Voice #2 . . . "With a whip!"

After we'd practiced crawling into the different positions a couple of times, our instructor drilled us on the three steps that would be involved in exiting the plane, when we would be doing this for real, 2,800 feet up in the sky. "Sit in the door. . . . Out on the strut. . . . Jump!"

Then we walked to another part of the field where we sat on the grass and listened to what the instructor had to say about hazards. "Some typical hazards you'll have to know how to deal with are corn fields, water, highways, trees, buildings, barbed-wire fences, power lines. . . ."

Power lines? My mind flashed an image of me fried black and dangling beside a lonely highway.

"If you see that you're going to come down into power lines and there's no way to avoid them," he said, "reach up and wrap your hands in the lines for insulation. Then make the rest of your body as skinny as you can, keep your feet together and pray like you've never prayed before."

Next came malfunctions, things that could go wrong with the parachute before we reached the ground (or the power lines, whichever came first). "There are three possible malfunctions," he told us, "the Mae West . . . the streamer . . . and the total."

Isn't there any good news? I wondered.

"A Mae West," he said, "occurs when one or more of the lines ends up over the top of the opened chute." "When that happens," he explained, "it looks

SOMETIMES YOU JUST HAVE TO STAND NAKED

like you're falling in a giant brassiere. A Mae West is dangerous because you'll be falling too fast and you won't have any control and you'll come in spinning and be screwed into the ground." (He had an odd sense of humor.)

"If you see that you have a Mae West," he continued, "open your reserve parachute casing . . . that's the chute you'll have strapped to your belly . . . being careful not to let any of it spill out. Then grab the folded chute with both hands and throw it as hard as you can in the direction you're spinning."

The first time I practiced that maneuver, hanging in a parachute harness from a wooden beam, I opened the reserve parachute casing, and the parachute spilled out like soft silk intestines onto the ground.

"No, no," the instructor yelled impatiently. "You've got to take ahold of the chute. If you let it spill out, it'll get wrapped around you and it won't open."

This was good advice, of course. But it was wasted on me; I knew I'd never have the presence of mind to follow it. If Mae West wanted me, I guessed she could have me.

Then the instructor slowly destroyed what little nerve I had left when he explained what we would have to do if we had either of the other malfunctions, the streamer and the total, when the main chute doesn't open at all.

I sat there for a while, thinking over my situation and barely listening to him. Then he stood up and said, "OK. Go over to the Quonset and find yourself a jump suit and a pair of boots."

Boots! That's it! Suddenly I had the perfect out; surely this little club wouldn't have any size 14 boots. And if I didn't have any boots, I wouldn't be allowed to jump.

Incredible as it still seems, there was one dusty pair of size 14 boots. Once again, my only hope was the wind.

After we were suited up (our jump suits were dingy work overalls), we were told to jump off a 3½-foot platform into pea gravel and practice the five-point roll: feet together, fall sideways to knees, then hip, back, shoulder, over and up . . . in one fluid movement. I was so fluid I half-sprained an ankle on my first try. This is how we were supposed to land at the end of the real jump. We practiced it frontward, backward, sideways . . . all the while the instructor repeating, "If you don't land right, you'll at least sprain an ankle and probably break a leg."

Throughout the five hours of instruction out there in that pasture, planes had been flying up whenever the wind allowed, and veteran skydivers had been jumping from as high as 8,200 feet and free-falling for thirty seconds. Each time I looked up and saw one of those little specks tumbling through the sky at about 100 miles an hour, I thought that his parachute had failed to open and he was surely going to land in a manner that would make me sick to my stomach. Then I'd see his chute billow out and a couple of seconds later hear a distinct "snap" as the delayed sound of its opening finally reached me. It was thrilling to watch them. Then I'd remember that my turn was coming and have another anxiety attack.

I had also spent a lot of time viewing the countryside, probably much the same way a soldier looks at a battlefield before the fighting begins. The country there east of Bardstown is beautiful. We were in a valley, surrounded by rolling shoulders of heavily treed hills.

Not a bad place to die, I thought.

By the time our instruction was finished, most of the clouds were gone and the wind had settled. We had all passed the written exam and signed forms saying we didn't hold Greene County Sport Parachute Center responsible for *anything.*

"Go find a helmet and get your chutes on," said our instructor. "It looks like you're gonna get to jump."

⌘　⌘　⌘　　　　　(to be continued)

Speaking of jumping, this looks like a good place to jump off my timid narrative for a while and move on to the subject of this chapter. But first, a. . . .

WRITING EXERCISE ─────────────────────────

Pick out someone (in class if that's where you're doing this) whose appearance interests you. Then observe that person closely and take notes, plan, write and rewrite a word portrait of him or her. Make it so detailed that an artist could create an accurate sketch from your description. As well as detailed descriptions of the person's height, build, hair, face, etc., describe such things as the way he or she moves, his or her gestures, facial expressions and general bearing. Be specific. Don't just say the person has brown eyes. Describe them. Are they dark, light, dull, glassy, bright, fiery? Are they close-set, deep-set, protruding? And show them in relation to the rest of the person's face: lashes, brows, lines, bags, nose, cheekbones, etc. Describe hair texture as well as color and length . . . skin color . . . smile . . . frown; don't miss anything.

Arrange your details in some logical order. You might open, for example, with the focus on whatever it is that's most noticeable about the person: nose, height, eyes, whatever. Then build your picture outward from there. Don't describe hair, then feet, then eyes, then weight; that's too jumpy and difficult to follow. Move from one detail to the next as if you're guiding the artist's pen.

DELIVERANCE FROM VAGUERY

In the last chapter, I talked about the importance of not only *showing* but showing *enough* . . . with details and/or examples. One of the things that skydiving story is supposed to do is illustrate effective use of *details.* I'm trying to give you enough of them so that you can see what I saw, hear what I heard, eavesdrop on what I thought and feel what I felt. If I do, you will understand what the experience meant to me.

Details are pieces of concrete information. Facts. And the more of them you use, the more likely you are to be understood. Use them and you'll be showing; don't use them and you'll be telling.

> The water glassed out for fifty yards ahead of us and went through an almost formal looking series of steep little cascades, changing into an even faster half-white half-green color, then through a short hook to the left where it shot between the big rocks.
>
> James Dickey
> *Deliverance*

> The water ahead was full of rapids.
>
> *Me*

Those are two ways of describing the same thing. But what a difference! Dickey's sentence recreates much more of the actual scene. As a result, it pulls alert readers deeper into the experience. It shows them what the writer saw. My sentence just tells them; it doesn't recreate it for them.

One principle to be learned from that: Sometimes it's not enough to simply give details. The details themselves must be detailed.

In my sentence, "rapids" is a detail of the river, and it does cause the reader to conjure up an image. But because the detail is general rather than specific, the writer has no control over what the reader imagines. One person reading my sentence might imagine a half-mile stretch of roaring rapids crashing over huge boulders. Another might imagine only slight or moderate disturbance in an otherwise gentle stream. If you want the readers to see it as *you* see it, give them enough details and make the details specific.

That's such an important point, I'm going to repeat it: Make your details specific. Not "The tree was bent" but "The tree leaned to the left." (If that tree is important enough to put in the writing, you might as well help the readers see it.) Not "She's tall" but "Her head comes to my chin and I'm six-foot-four" or "She's as tall as August corn" (must be a country girl) or "She's five-seven." (Don't overlook the obvious.)

Of course, in every experience there are countless details, and to try to include them all would wear out both the writer and the readers. Be selective. Give the readers enough details so they can clearly understand the experience you're recreating, and no more. And since one of your goals in any writing is to keep the readers interested, make sure the details you select are interesting ones.

Details that communicate sensory information (things that can be seen, heard, smelled, tasted, felt) are called *images*. All the images in that sentence from *Deliverance* are visual images, since they ask the readers to imagine seeing what the author is describing. An aural image (one that can be heard) would be something like "the fly buzzed" or "the car rattled" or "snap." Olfactory images (details that appeal to the sense of smell) are "the fishy odor of cat food" or "his hair smelled like cigarette smoke" or "rancid." "Sour grapes" and "bitter beer" appeal to the sense of taste. And "rough," "smooth" and "sharp" appeal to the sense of touch.

In addition to communicating sensory information (images), details can be used to recreate thoughts, personalities, attitudes, experiences . . . anything that contains facts.

LITERALLY OR FIGURATIVELY

Details can be presented either literally or figuratively. They are literal when they can be taken at face value, figurative when they can't. "The water glassed out" and "shot between the big rocks" are *figurative* details; water is not literally glass, nor can it literally shoot. Both details involve a descriptive comparison of one thing (water) with something with which it has something in common. The writer's purpose in doing this is to give the clearest picture he can. So instead of telling us that the water was *smooth*, he shows us *how* smooth it was: smooth as glass. And instead of telling us that the water flowed *swiftly* between the big rocks, he shows us *how* swiftly it was rushing: with the force of a shot.

Some *literal* details from Dickey's sentence: ". . . series of steep little cascades changing into a lighter color to go faster, and then into an even faster half-white half-green color. . . ." These are literal because they don't involve a comparison; they are simply statements of fact. It *is* a series of cascades and it *does* change colors as the water speeds up.

AMEN

As you develop your style and your sense of what needs to be said, concentrate first on describing details literally; describe them figuratively only when your literal vocabulary fails you. A healthy style is capable of using both, but it begins with a strong literal foundation.

WRITING EXERCISE _____

Using details from the physical description you're doing of a person, do a writing in which you show that person somewhere, doing something. This will be effective only if you use enough details so that the readers can see the person clearly, see the setting clearly, and see the action clearly.

Weave these three descriptions together rather than describing them a block at a time. Don't describe the person, then the place, then the activity. Instead, blend them, giving details of each as you go. You might begin with a brief picture of the person, then broaden the focus to show something of where he or she is, then begin the action, dropping in more details of the person and place as the action proceeds. Or, you might begin with description of the place, move your focus in for some description of the person, then begin the action. Or, you might begin with the action, and work in details of the person and place as the action moves along. However you do it, be sure when you're finished that the readers can see everything clearly.

This writing has the potential of being a story since you'll be working with three basic story elements . . . character, setting and action. You can also work in other story techniques, such as thought and dialogue. And you can include more than one character. Use your imagination.

❦   ❦   ❦

Tip #11

When you're describing or recalling something, try to avoid saying "I saw" . . . "I see" . . . "I could hear" . . . "I smell" . . . "I remember" . . . etc. If you hadn't seen it or heard it or tasted it or remembered it or whatever, you wouldn't be able to describe it. The readers know you saw it because they see you describing it.

One reason for following this advice is to eliminate unnecessary words. Another more important reason is to force yourself to be descriptive. For example, in the sentence "I heard a car," if you cut the "I heard" all you have left is "a car," and that's neither descriptive nor a sentence. To make it a sentence without saying "I heard," you'll have be be descriptive: "A car floated by, its tires humming a monotonous tune."

❦   ❦   ❦

Tip #12

Also try to avoid saying "there was" or "there is" or using any form of the verb "to be" when you're describing something. "There was an old barn on top of the hill." "There is a fly buzzing around my head." "Beside the rivulet there was a boulder covered with moss."

The forms of the verb "to be" (is, was, etc.) are not descriptive. You'll make your writing more descriptive . . . and interesting . . . if you'll cut the "there was" and replace it with a descriptive verb. "An old barn slouched on top of the hill." "A moss-covered boulder squatted beside the rivulet." Of course, look for the verb that describes what you see most accurately.

Sometimes a sentence can be improved by simply cutting the "there" and moving the "is" behind the subject. This puts the subject first and eliminates an unnecessary word. "A fly is buzzing around my head" is better than "There is a fly buzzing around my head." Bzzz.

❦   ❦   ❦

Tip #13

Stuck for an ending? Go back to the beginning. Seriously, that's a good place to find an ending. Don't just repeat a statement you made in the beginning, though. Instead, rephrase a key opening statement, or repeat or echo an image or word from the beginning that is central to what you're showing or explaining. This "circular" approach unifies the writing, and it lets the readers know that you haven't forgotten what you set out to do.

Another effective way to end is with a statement or short paragraph that puts everything in perspective.

If you have a good form for the piece you're writing, though, you probably won't have serious difficulty ending it, since the end is part of the form.

A DETAILED SICK JOKE

There were these two brothers who were students in a small college in Kentucky. Neither of them had ever won any awards for intelligence. One of them, the younger brother, was out driving one day, spaced out on something, lost control of the car, crashed through a fence, a utility pole and a barn before his car came to rest and burst into flames. When he drove through the utility pole he was decapitated, his head falling on the ground near the severed pole. The rest of his body burned to ashes in the fire. When the troopers arrived, all that was left of him was his head and his wallet, in which they found his identification.

Later, the other brother received a call from the morgue asking him to identify the remains. When he arrived, the attendant pulled back the sheet, revealing the brother's head, and asked, "Is this your brother?"

"No," he replied. "He was much taller than that."

ℐ ℐ ℐ

VOCABULARY EXERCISE #5

Look back through the writing you've produced so far in this course and pick out seven words whose meanings you're not absolutely certain of. Give *your* definition of each word . . . what you thought it meant when you used it. Then look up the dictionary's definition to see how to use it accurately. Use it accurately in a sentence. Then explain what you learned. As usual, do a word a day.

Sample

Word   scoot

My definition   to move sideways; to move quickly

Dictionary's definition to go or move quickly; hurry (off); dart

What I learned I had broadened the word's meaning and used it inaccu-
rately. "Sidle" means to move sideways.

Sentence I'm going to scoot out of here before the trouble starts.

⽊   ⽊   ⽊

STYLE SELF-ANALYSIS #2

If necessary, reread the explanation on page 50.

Sample

Strength I vary my sentence lengths.

Weakness I'm too wordy.

Corrective Study what the handbook says about wordiness, and cut every
word that's not absolutely necessary when I edit.

Deadline Two weeks from today.

Something else I intend to do to make my style more effective Study some
of my favorite author's styles more closely to see what makes them so
effective.

> Gonna buy me a '57 Buick
> and paint that mother green
> with a broom.
>
> *from the wall of a tavern*
> *john . . . a public journal*

CHAPTER 6

in which can be found the truth about america

from God Bless You, Mr. Rosewater
Kurt Vonnegut, Jr.

She was eighteen years old. She was an orphan from an orphanage that had been founded by the Buntline family in Pawtucket in 1878. When it was founded, the Buntlines required three things: That all orphans be raised as Christians, regardless of race, color, or creed, that they take an oath once a week before Sunday supper, and that, each year, an intelligent, clean female orphan enter domestic service in a Buntline home,

. . . in order to learn about the better things in life, and perhaps to be inspired to climb a few rungs of the ladder of culture and social grace.

The oath, which Selina had taken six hundred times, before six hundred very plain suppers, went like this, and was written by Castor Buntline, poor old Stewart's great-grandfather:

I do solemnly swear that I will respect the sacred private property of others, and that I will be content with whatever station in life God Almighty may assign me to. I will be grateful to those who employ me, and will never complain about wages and hours, but will ask myself instead, "What more can I do for my employer, my republic, and my God?" I understand that I have not been placed on Earth to be happy. I am here to be tested. If I am to pass the test, I must always be unselfish, always sober, always truthful, always chaste in mind, body, and deed, and always respectful to those whom God has, in His Wisdom, placed above me. If I pass the test, I will go to joy everlasting in Heaven when I die. If I fail, I shall roast in hell while the Devil laughs and Jesus weeps.

Selina, a pretty girl who played the piano beautifully and wanted to be a nurse, was writing to the head of the orphanage, a man named Wilfred Parrot. Parrot was sixty. He had done a lot of interesting things in his life, such as fighting in Spain in the Abraham Lincoln Brigade and, from 1933 until 1936, writing a radio serial called "Beyond the Blue Horizon." He ran a happy orphanage. All of the children called him "Daddy," and all of the children could cook and dance and play some musical instrument and paint.

Selena had been with the Buntlines a month. She was supposed to stay a year. This is what she wrote:

Dear Daddy Parrot: Maybe things will get better here, but I don't see how. Mrs. Buntline and I don't get along very well. She keeps saying I am ungrateful and impertinent. I don't mean to be, but I guess maybe I am. I just hope she doesn't get so mad at me she turns against the orphanage. That is the big thing I worry about. I am just going to have to try harder to obey the oath. What goes wrong all the time is things she sees in my eyes. She says something or does something I think is kind of dumb or pitiful or something, and I don't say anything about it, but she looks in my eyes and gets very mad. One time she told me that music was the most important thing in her life, next to her husband and her daughter. They have loudspeakers all over the house, all connected to a big phonograph in the front coat closet. There is music all day long, and Mrs. Buntline said what she enjoyed more than anything was picking out a musical program at the start of every day, and loading it into the record changer. This morning there was music coming out of all the loudspeakers, and it didn't sound like any music I had ever heard before. It was very high and fast and twittery, and Mrs. Buntline was humming along with it, rocking her head from side to side to show me how much she loved it. It was driving me crazy. And then her best friend, a woman named Mrs. Rosewater, came over, and she said how much she loved the music, too. I finally broke down and asked Mrs. Buntline what on earth it was. "Why, my dear child," she said, "that is none other than the immortal Beethoven." "Beethoven!" I said. "Have you heard of him before?" she said. "Yes, mam, I have. Daddy Parrot played Beethoven all the time back at the orphanage, but it didn't sound like that." So she took me in where the phonograph was, and she said, "Very well, I will prove it is Beethoven. I have loaded the changer with nothing but Beethoven. Every so often I just go on a Beethoven binge." "I just adore Beethoven, too," Mrs. Rosewater said. Mrs. Buntline told me to look at what was in the record changer and tell her whether it was Beethoven or not. It was. She had loaded the changer with all nine symphonies, but that poor woman had them playing at 78 revolutions per minute instead of 33, and she couldn't tell the difference. I told her about it, Daddy. I had to tell her, didn't I? I was very polite, but I must have gotten that look in my eyes, because she got very mad, and she made me go out and clean up the chauffeur's lavatory in the back of the garage. Actually, it wasn't a very dirty job. They haven't had a chauffeur for years.

Another time, Daddy, she took me out to watch a sailboat race in Mr. Buntline's big motorboat. I asked to go. I said all anybody ever seemed to talk about in Pisquontuit was sailboat races. I said I would like to see what was so wonderful about them. Her daughter Lila was racing that day. Lila is the best sailor in town. You should see all the cups she has won. They are the main

SOMETIMES YOU JUST HAVE TO STAND NAKED

decorations of the house. There aren't any pictures to speak of. A neighbor has a Picasso, but I heard him say he would a lot rather have a daughter who could sail like Lila. I don't think it makes much difference one way or another, but I didn't say so. Believe me, Daddy, I don't say half the things I could. Anyway, we went out to see this sailboat race, and I wish you could have heard the way Mrs. Buntline yelled and swore. You remember the things Arthur Gonsalves used to say? Mrs. Buntline used words that would have been news to Arthur. I never saw a woman get so excited and mad. She just forgot I was there. She looked like a witch with the rabies. You would have thought the fate of the universe was being decided by those sunburned children in those pretty little white boats. She finally remembered me, and she realized she had said some things that didn't sound very good. "You've got to understand why we're all so excited right now," she said. "Lila has two legs on the Commodore's Cup." "Oh," I said, "that explains everything." I swear, Daddy, that's all I said, but there must have been that look in my eyes.

What gets me most about these people, Daddy, isn't how ignorant they are, or how much they drink. It's the way they have of thinking that everything nice in the world is a gift to the poor people from them or their ancestors. The first afternoon I was there, Mrs. Buntline made me come out on the back porch and look at the sunset. So I did, and I said I liked it very much, but she kept waiting for me to say something else. I couldn't think of what else I was supposed to say, so I said what seemed like a dumb thing. "Thank you very much," I said. That was exactly what she was waiting for. "You're entirely welcome," she said. I have since thanked her for the ocean, the moon, the stars in the sky, and the United States Constitution.

Maybe I am just too wicked and dumb to realize how wonderful Pisquontuit really is. Maybe this is a case of pearls before swine, but I don't see how. I am homesick. Write soon. I love you.

Selena

P.S. Who really does run this crazy country?
     These creeps sure don't.

HOW SELENA MAKES IT CLEAR

A little way into her letter to Daddy Parrot, Selena made this general statement: "She says something or does something I think is kind of dumb or pitiful or something, and I don't say anything about it, but she looks in my eyes and gets very mad." Now, she could have stopped there and you would have had a general idea of what she was talking about. Instead, she recreated two experiences which exemplified what she meant by that general statement: Beethoven and sailboat racing. As a result, you know exactly what she meant. She made herself clear. She went beyond telling to showing.

Then, toward the end of her letter, she said, "What gets me most about these people . . . [is] the way they have of thinking that everything

nice in this world is a gift to the poor people from them or their ancestors."
And she went on to make her meaning clear with the sunset example.

Examples do more than make your writing clear; they can also help make it interesting. Each of Selena's examples is interesting in itself, while at the same time contributing to the interest value of the whole idea she's explaining to Daddy Parrot. Each example is a little story; at the same time it's part of a larger story.

AN "INTERESTING" DIGRESSION

The most effective writing is interesting as a whole . . . and interesting in each of its parts. A well-chosen word, a clear detail, a clear and appropriate example . . . each is interesting in itself while clarifying and giving life to the whole essay or story. Each makes the reader feel something and adds depth to the feeling developed by the whole.

Remember, "interesting" doesn't simply mean entertaining, though that's certainly one kind of interesting. We find interesting anything that makes us feel something . . . including writing that gives us things we can see clearly and somehow relate to our own experience.

Remember this too: Generalizations don't clarify, therefore they don't generate feelings; examples do.

FOR EXAMPLE

Usually, examples are short illustrations of something the writer is saying. They show what the writer means; they give a concrete picture. Examples can also be long, from paragraphs to pages. In a sense, a story, even a novel, is an example. It's a concrete illustration of a theme (general idea). After you read the story, you reflect on the idea that it exemplifies. My skydiving story could be read as an example of the general idea (theme) that taking risks fosters growth.

If you think about it, you can probably see how each of the suggested writings you've created so far is an example of something. Your sunset description is obviously an example of a sunset. It might be more than that, too, depending on what you wrote. It might be an example of the effect a sunset can have on a person who is observing it closely.

One way to insure that an experience you're planning to write about will be meaningful to your readers is to think of it as an example of something. For example, instead of simply recreating a frightening experience, think of it as an example of the way certain people (such as yourself) react to certain situations (such as the one that frightened you). In other words, try to see your own experience in a general perspective. While the readers may not be able to relate to the specific experience you're writing about, they will be able to relate to the general idea of which it is an example.

The same is true when you're writing about a person. Instead of simply recreating the person, think about what kind of people or behavior he or she exemplifies. Then you won't just be writing about your friend Horace but about something of which he is somehow an example. Sue Jarvis wasn't just writing about her mother (Chapter 4); she was writing about the effect a certain kind of mother (of which hers is an example) can have on a certain kind of child (of which Sue is an example).

I'm not saying that you should *tell* what your subject is an example of. I'm saying that you should see your subject as an example of something while you're planning how to present it. This will help you see what you need to include and what form to present it in. It will also give your writing focus. And it will make your writing meaningful and, therefore, interesting.

WRITING EXERCISE ─────────────────────────────

Make a general statement about yourself, something like, "While I was growing up, my mother filled me with so many of her fears that now I'm afraid of practically everything." Or, "My best asset is also my worst liability." Or, "I used to be late for everything until I learned my lesson." Or, "Sometimes my insecurity causes me to do some pretty bizarre things." Or, "More than anything else, I love the way driving fast makes me feel." Or, "It wasn't until I almost died that I began to appreciate life." Think about it for a while; what can you say about yourself that will allow you to use one or more interesting examples to explain it? When you've decided on your general statement, give enough interesting and detailed examples to show clearly what you mean. Or, give just one example, if it's enough to give a clear picture of what you mean.

After you've finished your rough draft, see if you can cut the generalization you started with. If you can, it's because your examples are clear enough that they speak for themselves. If you can't, it may mean that you need to do some more work on your examples. If you can't see any way to cut the general statement and still be understood, don't worry about it; maybe it's necessary.

The story that follows illustrates this approach. Bill begins with a general statement, which is the whole first paragraph. Then he tells a story which is, in effect, an example of what he said in the first paragraph.

The Day I Almost Became a Murder Victim
Bill Rummage

These days, unless a person is a member of S.W.A.T., or likes to play with nitroglycerin, it is seldom that he finds his life in immediate danger of ending. These are times, however, when suddenly and unexpectedly the tranquil lid is forced off the seal of the mind, exposing the limp thinking processes to a situation in which split-second thinking determines one's destiny. Such situations often evoke jitters, panic or terror in the unsuspecting individual. I know this because recently I suffered through all three in an experience in which my meager existence was threatened by violent acts.

As I reflect back to that day, I cannot help but remember the mild serenity that dominated my mind, as well as my friends', prior to the incident. The smooth calm of the pond water and the surrounding dark of the woods helped ease the tension that spring finals had so rudely brought upon us. Indeed, we had found the perfect outlet in a country pond, one that not only provided us with sunshine and fresh air, but with a tree swing that enabled us to fling through the air and into the water. Soon, after the remaining beers had been soaked up and some soft smoke inhaled, we found ourselves forgetting the drab atmosphere of college and orbiting into a world of our own. We plunged in and out of the water with all the exuberance of six Huckleberry Finns.

When the cars started pulling up near waterside, we had drifted well out into the pond. We looked upon the arrival of the cars with good favor, for it offered the prospect of the one commodity we were without . . . girls. Nevertheless, when no girls were seen stepping out of the cars, one of the more intoxicated members of our group welcomed the strangers by yelling "party" at them. When the only reply was a hoarse voice answering "no," we assumed that the strangers' and our intentions were of a different nature. Later, we knew this to be so when the same raspy voice informed us that he was going to drive my car into the pond.

The surprising announcement neither intimidated nor scared our group. After all, the situation from a certain viewpoint was funny, especially to my friends who often ridiculed me for being too carefree. Indeed, I had left the keys dangling in the ignition when we stopped to check out the pond. Now, because of my negligence, the stranger had the potential to destroy my car. With some apprehension, I started making my way toward shore. It was because of my apprehension, I suppose, that I let Smith Haynie come along with me.

Smith Haynie is a fine fellow. He was, scholastically speaking, one of the smarter freshmen attending Centre College. He had a 3.8 grade point average and prided himself on understanding people. His problem was that he was filthy rich and had been placed in European prep schools for the majority of his life. This did not benefit Smith in the development of levelheadedness, and thus he did not fully realize the fact that we were up against something more vicious than a textbook. As the two of us swam toward shore I found

SOMETIMES YOU JUST HAVE TO STAND NAKED

myself contrasting Smith's mechanical freestyle stroke with the wild characters we were about to encounter. He actually swam like the drivers drive in driver education films.

When the two of us reached shore, we were greeted by a crowd of unwelcome eyes. Haynie, displaying uncanny misinterpretation of what to do, asked for a customary hand out of the water. The request sparked hideous laughter from the crowd and prompted the leaders, including our hoarse-voiced friend, to harass Haynie. The scene was nonetheless beneficial to me. It enabled me to slip out of the water and grab the car keys without drawing any attention. Once I had the keys in my hand, I stayed ashore only long enough to see that the relatively large group of strangers were physically endowed and then I quickly made my way to the water. As I swam back I felt relief at having been spared a confrontation with the country boys because of my aristocratic friend. The relief was short-lived, however, when I turned to see Haynie being kicked in the face and then thrown into the pond. The jitters were beginning to set in.

Back in the company of my friends I sensed the sensation of shock that had momentarily overtaken our resourcefulness. As we treaded water waiting for the return of Haynie, we said little, but each knew what was on the others' minds. Being one to avoid trouble, especially with odds of four to one, I suggested that the six of us play it by ear from there, after swimming to the opposite shore. We swam doubly fast when Smith informed us that one of the strangers was toying with a shotgun.

Once on shore we discovered a gravel road that swerved into and around the woods. The road was located near the top of a slope some fifty yards above the water. By coincidence, this road joined the road on which we had parked the car. With Haynie insisting that the people on the other side were animals, and in light of what the hoarse leader had done to him, we decided to avoid the bullies by escaping down the road. However, there was a problem: we had no car. My car was parked alongside the ever-present bullies and the only camouflaged path to it involved a lengthy hike through the woods. Knowing this, and viewing the situation from all angles, we made the decision to send one of us after the car while the others waited to be picked up.

The question of who would pick up the car was decided by toss-of-the-coin elimination. When Smith Haynie lost and refused to go, I, being the runner up, made off for my car. The walk through the woods was long and lonely and difficult. As I neared the cars, and the sounds of the strangers became more vivid, I could not stop thinking about the movie *Deliverance*. Indeed, our situation superficially resembled the movie's, and, unfortunately for me, it was becoming more climactic each moment.

I paused to watch a white Chrysler drive away from the scene and to listen to alien voices. The fact that some of the group had left, I reasoned, indicated the possibility of the others leaving also. However, after a twenty-minute vigil, I decided this was not going to be. Thus, with the realization that things were not going to change unless I acted, I got up and, clenching my fists, walked briskly toward my car. The walk, surprisingly, was a short one, and as I came closer to a panoramic view I was delighted to see that the majority of the group was in the water. In fact, there were only three boys near the car. As I jerked my station wagon door open, the boys' heads jerked abruptly toward me. One of them yelled to the crowd below that the punk was trying to get away. My inconspicuous exit had been ruined. Grasping the steering wheel with sweaty palms, I noticed a couple of the bigger boys piling into a truck. The gravel flung wildly as both my car and the truck headed down the winding road. The chase was on.

Suddenly, in the midst of all this, I realized that my five companions might not be in their proper places. The thought, however, did not loom as big as the advancing truck. With each curve it moved a car size closer. Soon it was so close that I spotted two guns hanging in the rear window. Questions started popping in my head: Would they use the guns? Were they going to shoot at my tires, or were they going to take pot shots at me? Then everything went black. I jerked the wheel to the right and then to the left but to no avail. When the collision was over I felt a cold chill run down my spine. I had hit the white Chrysler.

It was then that I started to panic. As I opened the car door to examine the damage, I could see by the look of the strangers getting out of the truck that what I had done had been fully appreciated. One of them, who looked to be the youngest (perhaps my age), was laughing as if he expected to see more mishaps. The laughter was a bit perturbing, but the fact that the ominous bodies were keeping their distance was relieving as well as surprising. This made me think for an instant that I might escape the incident without conflict. That was before the facts started reeling through my mind. Although my station wagon had been virtually unscathed, the Chrysler front end had been mangled. Also, the strangers were violent and my friends were unable to be of any help since they were still waiting in the woods for my return.

Suddenly the hoarse bully and his friends appeared, walking up the slope. As the bully came closer I could hear him yelling something about his Chrysler and could see the Bowie knife in his hand. A pang of terror rose in my stomach.

As the bully neared, the first thing I noticed was his extreme ugliness. It did not seem in any way strange when one of his buddies called him "Rat." The name fit him. Before we could be properly introduced, the crowd formed a circle around the two of us. As he glanced at his car and then at me, I felt my back stiffen for the first time. Suddenly I was angered and appalled by the complete injustice of the whole situation. The thought of this thirty-year-old madman injuring or perhaps killing me and my friends was infuriating. So much so that I, standing in a situation tailor-made for Billy Jack, threatened them first. However, I reacted like Barney Fife when he started punching my face.

As the punches kept coming and my blood began to flow, I couldn't help thinking rather well of Rat for having thus far avoided using his knife. The punishment of the punches did not seem as painful as it did unusual. Soon, however, the murmur of the crowd signaled that the situation was about to worsen. Sure enough, Rat was pulling out his blade and coming for me.

At times like this one's adrenaline flow begins to accelerate. Quickly,

SOMETIMES YOU JUST HAVE TO STAND NAKED

perhaps instinctively, I made a run at the circle. Twice the large arms threw me back. On my third attempt I was held and forced to the ground. The situation had indeed worsened. As I stared at the knife above me I felt my life was about to end. Surely there was no escape, for Rat had assembled his knees upon my chest and with aid from his buddies had managed to restrain my arms. However, after I had been hit twice with the butt of the blade a voice rang out from the crowd. The words, "Hey, Rat, I want a piece of this sonofabitch," were in no way encouraging. But as I reflect back, they were perhaps the words that saved my skin.

The long-haired boy's plea was not appreciated by Rat. Again I felt terse knuckles graze my chin as Rat told him to stay back. Suddenly I was being assaulted not only in the face but in the ribs also as the boy sent a flurry of kicks into my side. This was clearly spoiling Rat's performance, so much so that he turned from me to shove the intruder away. The boy's intervention was causing a diversion. When one of the boys holding me got up to separate the two, my built up adrenaline burst into action; I flung off the other guardian and scurried through an opening in the crowd and into the freedom of the woods.

My journey through the woods was in every way pleasurable. As I dodged numerous trees I felt a strong sensation of freedom. Indeed, I had learned the meaning of Vince Lombardi's "run to daylight." The pressure of defending my life had been lifted and I felt eternally free. The relief was indescribable.

When I finally caught up with my friends, the police were with them. Smith Haynie had gotten to a phone and called the local police, the state police, the sheriff's department and the F.B.I. Efram Zimbalist, Jr., was the only one not present. Rat and some of his friends were arrested, and, of more importance, we were free to go.

On the way back to college, as I drove my car along the scattered white lines of the highway, I could not help noticing how beautiful the orange sky looked against the grayish landscape. Our leisure outing had turned into a frightening experience, but now that it was over I more fully appreciated the things life had given me.

❦ ❦ ❦

I first met Bill when he walked into my class early one summer wearing a face that was lumpy and grossly discolored. My ingenious greeting ("What happened to you?") led him to write the story you just read.

❦ ❦ ❦

Tip #14

I don't mean to take anything away from Bill's story, but notice that it could have gotten along perfectly well without its first paragraph. Before he started writing, he did what most of us do when trying to figure out how to tell about something that's important to us: he thought about it until he figured out what it all meant. Then he wrote that down and it became his first paragraph, his guide for telling the story.

The reason I say he could cut it is because he went on to tell the story so well that what it "meant" was clear and didn't need to be explained. He could also cut the first sentence of the second paragraph and begin his story with "The smooth calm of the pond water and the surrounding darkness of the woods. . . ."

When you edit and rewrite, you should consider cutting those generalizations with which you begin so many essays, stories, even paragraphs. Often they're necessary. But sometimes they're not; sometimes they're just guides for the writer, and the readers neither need nor want them.

While I'm hacking away at Bill's story, what do you think about his last sentence? Is it necessary? Would his story end more effectively without it?

MY BROTHER IS CRAZY

Because we are each unique, because the environment that shaped me is different from the environment that shaped you, we are always coming at things from different perspectives. Each of us is the result of his or her own experience of life.

Thus, no two people looking at the Grand Canyon see the same thing. Nor do two people listening to the same general statement hear the same thing. If I say to two people, "My brother is crazy," there will be three different versions of what I mean: mine and each of theirs. One of them might be reminded of his eccentric aunt who collected baseball cards and decorated her bedroom with *Playgirl* centerfolds. The other might be reminded of a deranged person who thought he was Richard Nixon.

If this is true, then complete communication, total understanding, between one human being and another is impossible. If everything I know, see and hear is filtered and distorted to conform to my concept of reality, and everything you know, see and hear is distorted to fit yours, how can we ever make contact? I don't think we can, completely. But that's no reason to stop trying. In fact, it's a reason for trying harder. In a sense, that's what communication is all about: one human being trying to make meaningful contact with another.

And the more concrete I can make what I'm talking about, the closer I'll come to being understood. That's where details and examples come in. They help make the abstract concrete, the general specific, the vague clear.

A general statement tells the readers what I have in mind generally;

SOMETIMES YOU JUST HAVE TO STAND NAKED

an example shows them what I have in mind specifically. Without examples, the readers are left with only a vague idea of what I'm talking about. Worse yet, by supplying their own examples to fill the information gap, they may end up thinking something entirely different from what I intended. Take the statement "My brother is crazy," for example. Both of the people I said that to will continue to think of eccentric aunts and psychotic Richard Nixons until I show them, with examples of his behavior, what I mean when I say my brother is crazy.

As a general rule, when you write a generalization be willing to clarify it with an example.

Ed: What word describes a successful dieter?

Me: Uh . . . oh, I don't know.

Ed: Ex-ample. Yuk. Yuk.

Me: ?

Ed: What did the Indian say after he'd gathered a whole basketful of eggs?

Me: I don't know, Ed.

Ed: Eggs ample. Yuk. Yuk.

Me: Ed. . . .

Ed: Yeah?

Me: Why are you doing this?

Ed: Don't you get it? Ex-ample? Eggs ample? I was just giving you a funny finish for what you've been talking about in this chapter. Examples. Yuk. Yuk.

Me: Really funny, Ed. Really funny.

Ed: Thanks. Hey! What're you putting on my head?

Me: Oh, that's just an egg sample. Snicker.

Ed: Yuck!

☙   ☙   ☙

Tip #15

Avoid using the word "so" as an adverb. It doesn't say anything specific. "I'm so tired." "It's so beautiful." How tired is "so" tired? How beautiful is "so" beautiful? Using "so" like that is admitting you're too lazy to think for the words that would express what you mean exactly. Use "so" only if you intend to complete the idea that it begins: "I'm so angry I could spit!" "I was so happy I cried." "Her eyes were so beautiful I couldn't look into them and talk at the same time."

& & &

Tip #16

Avoid using the words "very" and "really." Eliminate them from your writing vocabulary (except when you need them to sound natural, as in dialogue). In most cases, as with "so," we use those words when we're too lazy to think for the words that would express what we mean exactly. It's easier to say "This book is really good" or "This book is very good" than to come up with the word that precisely expresses my opinion of it. How good is "really" good? How pretty is "very" pretty? At best, those words give a general idea. But what good is that?

In other cases, when you have come up with a word that precisely expresses your meaning, tacking on a "very" or a "really" weakens, rather than strengthens, what you're saying. For example, to say that someone is "unique" is clear and precise. To say that the person is "very unique" or "really unique" sticks the readers with an unnecessary word and therefore draws their attention away from the important word. Let precise words like "unique" do the job they were invented to do.

A good general rule is to try to avoid adverbs altogether. They're seldom necessary if your verbs and adjectives are precise.

& & &

SUGGESTED PUBLIC WRITING #3

If you don't already have something you care to write about, consider this: Write about someone who has had a definite and demonstrable effect on you. For example, it might be someone who affected your attitude toward yourself, or your sense of humor, or your belief in God, or the way you look at nature or other people, or your decision not to steal cars anymore. Or, the influence might be more general. In any case, show the person and show his or her effect on you.

Purpose. To show how one person, through words and/or example, can affect another . . . and probably also to hold this person up as some kind of example, good or bad.

Audience. The readers of an appropriate publication and/or people who would somehow benefit from such an example.

Form. Try recreating the experience(s) that brought on the change in you, showing what this person was like, what you were like together and what you were like before and after the change.

⁞ ⁞ ⁞

ED'S ALTERNATE

Rhetorically, you have a couple of possibilities on that one: either cause-effect analysis or comparison and contrast. Either you concentrate on showing how this person (the cause) changed you (the effect), or you concentrate on showing what you were like before and after the person's influence (comparison and contrast). I've already explained the usefulness of cause-effect analysis, so I'll suggest you work with comparison and contrast on this writing. How about comparing and contrasting two or more *places*, say for their desirability as places to vacation? Or you could compare and contrast two or more types of people, say on the basis of their suitability as mates or teachers or friends.

⁞ ⁞ ⁞

VOCABULARY EXERCISE #6

At the usual rate of one-a-day-for-seven-days, pick out of your writings verbs and adjectives that you use accurately and enjoy using. Then look in your thesaurus to find a useful alternative for each one. Use your dictionary to define the alternative. And use it in an imaginative sentence. Use the usual word-definition-sentence format.

> The people who see miracles
> are the people who look for
> miracles, the people who
> open their eyes to the
> miracles that surround
> us always. The people
> who have routine flights
> are the people who believe
> they are on routine flights.
>
> Tom Robbins
> *Even Cowgirls Get the Blues*

CHAPTER 7

have you ever felt like a wounded cow?

have you ever felt like a wounded cow
halfway between an oven and a pasture?
walking in a trance toward a pregnant
seventeen-year-old housewife's
two-day-old cookbook?

Richard Brautigan

Ed: Ahem. . . .

Me: Oh . . . hi, Ed. You're not still angry about that egg sample, are you?

Ed: No.

Me: Good. Well, what can I do for you?

Ed: It's the title of this chapter.

Me: What's wrong with it?

Ed: There are *thirty* words in it! Thirty-two if you count "Richard Brautigan."

Me: So?

Ed: So, you said back in Tip #10 that a good title has. . . .

Me: I know . . . I know, five words or less.

Ed: Right.

Me: But I also said that length is the *last* consideration, after interest and relevance. I know you can't see its relevance yet, but don't you think it's interesting?

Ed: Oh, sure, it's interesting. Sort of. But thirty words?

Me: Look, Ed . . . whose book is this?

Ed: Well . . . yours . . . but. . . .

Me: Right.

Ed: But. . . .

Me: You need to loosen up, Ed. Here, have some more Brautigan. He's good for that.

The Kool-Aid Wino
Richard Brautigan

When I was a child I had a friend who became a Kool-Aid wino as the result of a rupture. He was a member of a very large and poor German family. All the older children in the family had to work in the fields during the summer, picking beans for two-and-one-half cents a pound to keep the family going. Everyone worked except my friend who couldn't because he was ruptured. There was no money for an operation. There wasn't even money to buy him a truss. So he stayed home and became a Kool-Aid wino.

One morning in August I went over to his house. He was still in bed. He looked up at me from underneath a tattered revolution of old blankets. He had never slept under a sheet in his life.

"Did you bring the nickel you promised?" he asked.

"Yeah," I said. "It's here in my pocket."

"Good."

He hopped out of bed and he was already dressed. He had told me once that he never took off his clothes when he went to bed.

"Why bother?" he had said. "You're only going to get up, anyway. Be prepared for it. You're not fooling anyone by taking your clothes off when you go to bed."

He went into the kitchen, stepping around the littlest children, whose wet diapers were in various stages of anarchy. He made his breakfast: a slice of homemade bread covered with Karo syrup and peanut butter.

"Let's go," he said.

We left the house with him still eating the sandwich. The store was three blocks away, on the other side of a field covered with heavy yellow grass. There were many pheasants in the field. Fat with summer they barely flew away when we came up to them.

"Hello," said the grocer. He was bald with a red birthmark on his head. The birthmark looked just like an old car parked on his head. He automatically reached for a package of grape Kool-Aid and put it on the counter.

"Five cents."

"He's got it," my friend said.

I reached into my pocket and gave the nickel to the grocer. He nodded and the old red car wobbled back and forth on the road as if the driver were having an epileptic seizure.

We left.

My friend led the way across the field. One of the pheasants didn't even bother to fly. He ran across the field in front of us like a feathered pig.

When we got back to my friend's house the ceremony began. To him the making of Kool-Aid was a romance and a ceremony. It had to be performed in an exact manner and with dignity.

First he got a gallon jar and we went around to the side of the house where the water spigot thrust itself out of the ground like the finger of a saint, surrounded by a mud puddle.

He opened the Kool-Aid and dumped it into the jar. Putting the jar under the spigot, he turned the water on. The water spit, splashed and guzzled out of the spigot.

He was careful to see that the jar did not overflow and the precious Kool-Aid spill out onto the ground. When the jar was full he turned the water off with a sudden but delicate motion like a famous brain surgeon removing a disordered portion of the imagination. Then he screwed the lid tightly onto the top of the jar and gave it a good shake.

The first part of the ceremony was over.

Like the inspired priest of an exotic cult, he had performed the first part of the ceremony well.

His mother came around the side of the house and said in a voice filled with sand and string, "When are you going to do the dishes? . . . Huh?"

"Soon," he said.

"Well, you better," she said.

When she left, it was as if she had never been there at all. The second part of the ceremony began with him carrying the jar very carefully to an abandoned chicken house in the back. "The dishes can wait," he said to me. Bertrand Russell could not have stated it better.

He opened the chicken house door and we went in. The place was littered with half-rotten comic books. They were like fruit under a tree. In the corner was an old mattress and beside the mattress were four quart jars. He took the gallon jar over to them and filled them carefully not spilling a drop. He screwed their caps on tightly and was now ready for a day's drinking.

You're supposed to make only two quarts of Kool-Aid from a package, but he always made a gallon, so his Kool-Aid was a mere shadow of its desired potency. And you're supposed to add a cup of sugar to every package of Kool-Aid, but he never put any sugar in his Kool-Aid because there wasn't any sugar to put in it.

He created his own Kool-Aid reality and was able to illuminate himself by it.

from *Trout Fishing in America*

U + S + F = IW

I've read that story at least thirty times, and it's never failed to delight me. It's ten minutes of Brautigan at his best: funny, laid back, unusual.

Even when I'm not reading it, I frequently think about it. And when I do, I always remember that birthmark on the grocer's forehead, the fat pheasants, the comic books in the old chicken house and the entire last sentence. I remember the birthmark, the pheasants and the comic books because they are interesting details.

There are several things about them that make them interesting. For one thing, each is a visual detail (*image*); I can picture it in my mind. In addition, each detail is *unusual*, something I either haven't seen before or don't give much thought or attention to. And finally, each is interesting because it is presented *figuratively*. I remember the birthmark because Brautigan showed me what it looked like: an old car parked on the grocer's bald head. I remember the pheasants because he described one as looking like a feathered pig. And I remember the comic books because he described them as littering the floor of the old chicken house like fruit under a tree.

There's a formula there for interesting writing: If you want your readers to understand and enjoy reading about your experience, include some unusual details, and make them appeal to your readers' senses, figuratively if possible.

U (unusual) + S (senses) + F (figurative) = IW (interesting writing). (I should have been an algebraist.) If you can hold your readers' interest with your details, they're more likely to be interested in the whole experience you're sharing with them.

I also mentioned that I remember the entire last sentence of "The Kool-Aid Wino": "He created his own Kool-Aid reality and was able to illuminate himself by it." (See. I remember the whole thing.) It's memorable because it's thought-provoking; it makes me think not only about the story but also about how it explains a lot besides the story. I think we each create our own reality and illuminate ourselves by it. One mark of a good writer is that he or she gives you interesting things to think about. Thanks, Brautigan.

❧ ❧ ❧

KOOL-AID REALITY RECIPE QUIZ. Normal Kool-Aid reality is made with two quarts of water and one cup of sugar. The Kool-Aid wino creates his with four quarts of water and no sugar. How much water and how much sugar do you use to create *your* Kool-Aid reality?

ANALOGIES

Analogies are comparisons. Not just any comparisons, though: figurative comparisons; they talk about one thing as if it were something else. Some analogies are *stated* comparisons (similes); some are *implied* comparisons (metaphors).

Both analogies and literal details (Chapter 5) are means to the same ends: clarity and interest. Writers use one or the other or both, depending on their needs. If what they want to communicate can be best communicated literally, they'll give you the details literally. If it can be best explained figuratively, they'll give you the details figuratively. Most effective writing contains a mixture of both.

Though good writers sometimes use analogies for the fun of it, they normally use them because they can explain what they're trying to explain better with them. As far as they can tell, nothing they might say literally will do as well in that particular situation. They also use analogies because analogies say (and imply) more, in fewer words, than most literal explanations. And, like the rest of us, they use them for one more reason: Our language contains around a million words, but not even that many is enough to describe and explain all that we experience. Experiences, feelings, sensations are often almost impossible to explain literally. That's why you frequently find yourself using a comparison to make yourself clear. And your comparisons are usually figurative: "She was a real fox." "He was as skinny as a toothbrush." "Her brain was on vacation, but her mouth was working overtime."

Unfortunately, most of the analogies we use in normal conversation are less than satisfactory for writing. Their surprise value and clarity have dulled from years of overuse. (See Tip #17.) Because it's easy for most readers' interest to wander, as a writer you have to *work* to keep their attention. One way to keep it is to use fresh analogies, ones you've created yourself.

A PHEASANT IS NOT A PIG

Analogies make comparisons between things that normally don't seem to have anything in common. (What do a pheasant and a pig have in common?) And the comparisons usually rest on only one likeness. For example, when Brautigan compared the pheasant to a pig, he only meant that the fat pheasant looked and moved like a pig when it ran, and not that it had a flat snout, a curly tail and ears out of which silk purses could not be made.

Comparisons of things that have *much* in common . . . such as "Her hair was blonde like her mother's" . . . are not analogies but *literal* comparisons. They tell the truth directly rather than coming at it through what is, in a sense, a lie. (A pheasant is not a pig.)

Descriptions by analogy are usually more effective than literal details because analogies stimulate the readers' imaginations and give them a new way of looking at or thinking about something. Because a story I read described a deer's tail as a white flag, every time I see a deer's tail from now on I'll see a flag. Because Brautigan described the disorder of the Kool-Aid wino's bed as a "tattered revolution of old blankets," I now have a new perspective on the disarray of my own kids' beds.

AN ACE-IN-THE-HOLE NOVELTY. DO YOU WANT TO BE THE *LIFE* OF THE POKER GAME? THE MOST *POPULAR* POKER PLAYER IN TOWN? YOU'LL BE A REAL *WINNER,* A FIRST RATE JOKER, WHEN YOU DEAL OUT ANY OF THE HUNDREDS OF CLEVER SIMILES AND METAPHORS CONTAINED IN THIS FANTASTIC NEW BOOK: *AN ANALOGY FOR EVERY HAND.* IMAGINE THE RESPECT YOU'LL COMMAND. HERE ARE TWO OF THE CLEVER QUIPS YOU'LL BE MAKING IN NO TIME AT ALL:

When you're drawing good cards: "I'm drawin' like a depot stove."

When you're losing: "I'm goin' down like a one-egg pudding."

DON'T DELAY. SEND YOUR CHECK TODAY TO: ACE-IN-THE-HOLE NOVEL-TIES, LAS VEGAS, NEVADA. AT ONLY $7.11, HOW CAN YOU LOSE?

SIMILES

A simile is a stated or expressed comparison. It explains one thing by saying that it is *like* something else. It uses words such as "like," "as," "similar to," "than" and "resembles" to state the comparison. The loser and the winner in that poker silliness above both used similes. Brautigan used similes to describe the birthmark, the pheasant and the comic books. Here are a few more similes from *Trout Fishing in America.* They're a bit elaborate; read them slowly and think about them.

The sun was like a huge fifty-cent piece that someone had poured kerosene on and then had lit with a match and said, "Here, hold this while I go get a newspaper," and put the coin in my hand, but never came back.

The girl was very pretty and her body was like a clear mountain river of skin and muscle flowing over rocks of bone and hidden nerves.

One April morning we were standing around in the play yard, acting as if it were a huge open-air pool hall with the first-graders coming and going like pool balls.

When we reached Stanley, the streets were white and dry like a collision at a high rate of speed between a cemetery and a truck loaded with sacks of flour.

WRITING EXERCISE ———————————————————————————

Look at something, listen to something, smell something, taste something, feel something. Describe each sensation in writing so that your readers can see it, hear it, smell it, taste it and feel it the same as you did. In each description use at least one simile.

Don't use similes you've heard or read somewhere, though; create your own for the occasion . . . and make them accurate. Creating original similes (or metaphors) is not as difficult as some people seem to think. All you have to do is think a little harder than usual, and let your imagination out to play. The perfect comparison is there; you just have to find it.

Ideally, your simile will not only describe your subject physically, but will also suggest something about its nature or essence. For example, you *could* say that a street was as white as snow. That might describe it physically but it doesn't suggest anything about its nature. Brautigan's white street simile above both describes it and reminds you of a street's connection with death.

If you're feeling ambitious, try using all five senses to describe a single item or scene . . . or a person that you wouldn't mind smelling, tasting and feeling. (Aren't senses wonderful!)

METAPHORS

A metaphor is an implied comparison. In a sense, it is a simile without the word "like" or "as." Usually, though, a metaphor is more forceful than a simile. It makes a statement that is literally untrue; it says that one thing *is* another. ("It's raining cats and dogs" says that the falling water is cats and dogs.) A metaphor is more forceful because it doesn't come right out like a simile and tell you that it's comparing one thing to another; it merely *implies* that it is. This forces the readers to work a little harder than they do to interpret a simile. They must first realize that the writer is not insane but making a comparison. Then they must understand what's being compared to what. Then they must perceive the connection. With a good metaphor, the readers will do all of this thinking instantaneously and effortlessly, though they may be so intrigued by this new insight that they will stop reading and dwell on it for a while. When the readers do that, you have them.

"Her brain was on vacation, but her mouth was working overtime" is a metaphor . . . an interesting way of saying there was nothing of interest on her mind but she didn't let that stop her from talking, and talking. These are metaphors, too: "If I don't get to sleep soon, I'll be a bear in the morning." "The leaves waltzed over the ground." "A sea of children flooded the candy store." "Her smile fell to the floor and shattered when she understood what I was saying."

At the risk of belaboring the obvious (beating a dead horse), let me explain why a couple of those are metaphors.

"I'll be a bear in the morning" is a metaphor because it implies a comparison between myself and a bear when we haven't had sufficient sleep: grumpy, mean, a real pain to be around. It would have been a simile (stated comparison) if I'd said "I'll be *like* a bear." It would be literal if I said "I'll be grumpy, mean, a real pain. . . ."

"The leaves waltzed over the ground" implies a comparison between the way the leaves are moving in the wind and the way people look when they waltz: rhythmic, graceful, in unison. (I saw some leaves today *hustling* across the street. Get it?)

Enough explanation? Good. Here are some metaphors from *Trout Fishing in America:*

. . . wet diapers in various stages of *anarchy.* . . . (instead of something literal like "various stages of disorder")

Fat with *summer.* . . . (instead of something literal like "fat and lazy from all the food and warmth of summer")

To him the making of Kool-Aid was a *romance* and a *ceremony.* . . .

. . . a voice filled with *sand* and *string.* . . .

. . . his Kool-Aid was a mere *shadow* of its desired potency. . . .

I walked down past the glass *whiskers* of the houses, reflecting the downward rushing *waterfalls* of night. . . .

WRITING EXERCISE

Follow the same instructions as for the Writing Exercise on similes. But this time, instead of using a simile in each description, use a metaphor. And use different objects, scenes or persons for this exercise than you used for the other one.

THE LONG . . .

An analogy (simile or metaphor) can be long, carrying the comparison through a paragraph, a chapter or an entire book. Here's a one-paragraph metaphor from *Trout Fishing in America:*

I fished upstream coming ever closer and closer to the narrow staircase of the canyon. Then I went up into it as if I were entering a department store. I caught three trout in the lost and found department. . . . We ended up at a large pool that was formed by the creek crashing through the children's toy section.

Some people claim not to like that kind of writing. They say it's too flowery, or it's confusing, or it's just silly. I say, "Don't be such an *Ed.*" For one thing, it's funny. Maybe not slap-your-knee funny, but at least tickle-your-imagination-and-make-you-smile funny. And it's not just some off-the-wall comparison; there's a point to it. It not only gives the readers an image of the place where the narrator was fishing, it suggests the manner in which he was fishing: shopping around. And it suggests the mood he was in: like some people feel while roaming through a large department store. Plus, "the lost and found department" implies (to me) a quiet, out-of-the-way part of the river, while "the children's toy section" implies a lively, colorful area.

That's the way accurate analogies work . . . when you allow them to work on you: they suggest and imply all sorts of interesting things about what the writer is explaining.

If you're one of those people who don't like that kind of writing, you're going to hate the following excerpt. It carries the comparison, "The creek was like 12,845 telephone booths in a row," through an entire chapter, which Brautigan titled . . .

The Hunchback Trout
Richard Brautigan

The creek was made narrow by little green trees that grew too close together. The creek was like 12,845 telephone booths in a row with high Victorian ceilings and all the doors taken off and all the backs of the booths knocked out.

Sometimes when I went fishing in there, I felt just like a telephone repairman, even though I did not look like one. I was only a kid covered with fishing tackle, but in some strange way by going in there and catching a few trout, I kept the telephones in service. I was an asset to society.

It was pleasant work, but at times it made me uneasy. It could grow dark in there instantly when there were some clouds in the sky and they worked their way onto the sun. Then you almost needed candles to fish by, and foxfire in your reflexes.

Once I was in there when it started raining. It was dark and hot and steamy. I was of course on overtime. I had that going in my favor. I caught seven trout in fifteen minutes.

The trout in those telephone booths were good fellows. There were a lot of young cutthroat trout about six to nine inches long, perfect pan size for local calls. Sometimes there were a few fellows, eleven inches or so—for the long distance calls.

I've always liked cutthroat trout. They put up a good fight, running against the bottom and then broad jumping. Under their throats they fly the orange banner of Jack the Ripper.

Also in the creek were a few stubborn rainbow trout, seldom heard from, but there all the same, like certified public accountants. I'd catch one every once in a while. They were fat and chunky, almost as wide as they were long. I've heard those trout called "squire" trout.

It used to take me about an hour to hitchhike to that creek. There was a river nearby. The river wasn't much. The creek was where I punched in. Leaving my card above the clock, I'd punch out again when it was time to go home.

I remember the afternoon I caught the hunchback trout.

A farmer gave me a ride in a truck. He picked me up at a traffic signal beside a bean field and he never said a word to me.

His stopping and picking me up and driving me down the road was as automatic a thing to him as closing the barn door, nothing need be said about it, but still I was in motion traveling thirty-five miles an hour down the road, watching houses and groves of trees go by, watching chickens and mailboxes enter and pass through my vision.

Then I did not see any houses for a while. "This is where I get out," I said.

The farmer nodded his head. The truck stopped.

"Thanks a lot," I said.

The farmer did not ruin his audition for the Metropolitan Opera by making a sound. He just nodded his head again. The truck started up. He was the original silent old farmer.

A little while later I was punching in at the creek. I put my card above the clock and went into that long tunnel of telephone booths.

I waded about seventy-three telephone booths in. I caught two trout in a little hole that was like a wagon wheel. It was one of my favorite holes, and always good for a trout or two.

I always like to think of that hole as a kind of pencil sharpener. I put my reflexes in and they came back out with a good point on them. Over a period of a couple of years, I must have caught fifty trout in that hole, though it was only as big as a wagon wheel.

I was fishing with salmon eggs and using a size 14 single egg hook on a pound and a quarter test tippet. The two trout lay in my creel covered entirely by green ferns, ferns made gentle and fragile by the damp walls of telephone booths.

The next good place was forty-five telephone booths in. The place was at the end of a run of gravel, brown and slippery with algae. The run of gravel dropped off and disappeared at a little shelf where there were some white rocks.

One of the rocks was kind of strange. It was a flat white rock. Off by itself from the other rocks, it reminded me of a white cat I had seen in my childhood.

The cat had fallen or been thrown off a high wooden sidewalk that went along the side of a hill in Tacoma, Washington. The cat was lying in a parking lot below.

The fall had not appreciably helped the thickness of the cat, and then a few people had parked their cars on the cat. Of course, that was a long time ago and the cars looked different from the way they look now.

You hardly ever see those cars anymore. They are the old cars. They have to get off the highway because they can't keep up.

That flat white rock off by itself from the other rocks reminded me of that dead cat come to lie there in the creek, among 12,845 telephone booths.

I threw out a salmon egg and let it drift down over that rock and WHAM! a good hit! and I had the fish on and it ran hard downstream, cutting at an angle and staying deep and really coming on hard, solid and uncompromising, and then the fish jumped and for a second I thought it was a frog. I'd never seen a fish like that before.

God-damn! What the hell!

The fish ran deep again and I could feel its life energy screaming back up the line to my hand. The line felt like sound. It was like an ambulance siren coming straight at me, red light flashing, and then going away again and then taking to the air and becoming an air-raid siren.

The fish jumped a few more times and it still looked like a frog, but it didn't have any legs. Then the fish grew tired and sloppy, and I swung and splashed it up the surface of the creek and into my net.

The fish was a twelve-inch rainbow trout with a huge hump on its back. A hunchback trout. The first I'd ever seen. The hump was probably due to an injury that occurred when the trout was young. Maybe a horse stepped on it or a tree fell over in a storm or its mother spawned where they were building a bridge.

There was a fine thing about that trout. I only wish I could have made a death mask of him. Not of his body though, but of his energy. I don't know if anyone would have understood his body. I put it in my creel.

Later in the afternoon when the telephone booths began to grow dark at the edges, I punched out of the creek and went home. I had that hunchback trout for dinner. Wrapped in cornmeal and fried in butter, its hump tasted sweet as the kisses of Esmeralda.

from Trout Fishing in America

⅋   ⅋   ⅋

What details do you remember from that story? I remember a stream that looked like 12,845 Victorian telephone booths, the original silent old farmer, a rock that looked like a flat white cat, and a hunchback trout whose hump tasted as sweet as the kisses of Esmeralda. Yum.

... AND THE SHORT OF IT

Most effective analogies are not elaborate comparisons but single words, usually verbs and adjectives. They provide quick, often brilliant clarity, insight, perspective. For example: "The wind *screamed* through the shutters." "Frost *engraved* the windows." "His *crumbling* nerve. . . ." "A *curtain* of fog. . . ." And these, from *Trout Fishing in America:*

> *. . . child-eyed* rats. . . .

> They both looked very *sheepish,* caught in the *teeth* of the flashlight.

The use of descriptive (meaning "accurate," not "showy") words, whether literal or figurative, can mean the difference between dull writing and interesting writing . . . writing that bores the readers and writing that keeps their mental eyes open. Consider the difference between "He climbed the ladder" and "He struggled up the ladder," "I went to class" and "I trudged to class," "The sun came up" and "The sun yawned and rose slowly out of the trees," "The bus went by" and "The bus farted up the street."

Descriptive words, especially analogies, will make your style more colorful and therefore more interesting. They will also make it more precise. But most of all they will make your style more individual because the analogies you create are clear evidence of how *you* perceive things.

⊗ ⊗ ⊗

Tip #17

Clichés are worn-out expressions like "I feel like hell" . . . "as cute as a button" . . . "slept like a log" . . ."raining cats and dogs" . . . "beating a dead horse." Most clichés were fresh similes and metaphors at one time, but they have been used so much that they are no longer effective. Thus, you should avoid using them in your writing. Good writing is fresh; it keeps the readers alert. Clichés lull them to sleep or allow their minds to wander from what you're saying. But the best reason for not using a cliché to describe or explain something is that it doesn't show the way *you* saw it; rather it describes how the person who first created that analogy (before it was a cliché) saw it. Be yourself. Look, listen, feel, etc. with an open mind, not one filled with other people's words and perceptions.

⊗ ⊗ ⊗

Tip #18

Analogies, like literal descriptions, must be accurate to be effective. Never settle for a simile or metaphor that *almost* describes the way you saw or understood something. Look at it and think about it until you can create an analogy that expresses it as exactly as possible. The results will be worth the effort, both for your writing and for your readers.

❀ ❀ ❀

VOCABULARY EXERCISE #7

Go back through the thirty-five words you've selected so far for your Vocabulary Exercises and, at the usual rate of one a day, pick out seven words that you haven't used yet, either for thinking, talking or writing. Replace them with ones you *know* you can use. Employ the usual word-definition-sentence format.

❀ ❀ ❀

STYLE SELF-ANALYSIS #3

If necessary, reread the directions on page 50. And notice that something's been added (*).

Sample

Strength   I'm using more original analogies.

Weakness   I use the word "thing" too much.

Corrective   Each time it comes up, try to think of a more precise alternative.

Deadline   Immediately.

Something else I'm doing to make my style more effective   Browsing through my handbook, reviewing the rules.

**Weakness that's already been corrected*   I don't use confusing sentence fragments any more.

> . . . All a person can do in this life
> is to gather about him his integrity,
> his imagination and his individuality . . .
> and with these ever with him, out front
> and in sharp focus, leap into the dance
> of experience.
>
> Tom Robbins
> *Even Cowgirls Get the Blues*

CHAPTER 8

the conoitions of a solitary biro

A Solitary Bird, Part IV

I sat alone on the end of a green picnic table. My main and reserve parachutes were harnessed securely. My helmet rested in my lap. As I waited for our jump master to tell us when to board the plane, I wandered back to December 29, 1963, for a closer look at something that had been lurking in the back of my mind all day.

I was twenty-one then, a senior in college, home for Christmas break. It was 2:00 A.M. I was standing behind my car, which I had pushed half off the four-lane, one-way street, trying to slop gas out of an antifreeze can into my empty tank. Another car was parked behind me, its lights on to help me see. I was cold. I was mad at my brother for leaving me a car with only enough gas to take me six blocks. I was thinking about what I was going to say to Suzi when I took her home. We had met in August; tonight I was going to break up with her. I was going to Nassau over spring break and Europe in the summer. I was going to be free for a while. But before I had dribbled half a gallon of gas into the tank a drunk driver screeched out of the night into the car behind me and nearly severed my right leg between the bumpers.

At the hospital, our family doctor looked at all the bone splinters, gas and gravel in my leg and said it might have to be amputated. But the orthopedic surgeon thought he could save it.

After I'd spent a month in the hospital and three more at home, x-rays showed that the bone ends were dying rather than healing. So the doctor performed a bone graft. Six months and two casts later, he told me it was healed. A few days after that I went to my cousin's wedding reception. When I awoke the next morning my leg was broken again.

And again it refused to heal. So there was another bone graft, followed by nine more months of casts. Then I was fitted for a leg brace, a thick leather cuff that laced from my knee to my ankle. A stainless steel rod ran down each side and attached to the heel of my shoe. I hated that brace. When I was on crutches, people would ask me what had happened. But now that I was in a shiny, clunky brace, they stopped asking. They no longer found my affliction interesting or humorous. I guess they figured I had polio and didn't want to embarrass me by showing they'd noticed.

On New Year's Eve, 1965, I went to a party and left the brace at home. At 2:30 in the morning I was carried out of the party with my arms over the shoulders of two friends, my leg broken again.

I was despondent; the doctor was furious. Two years . . . three operations . . . wasted. When he calmed down, he said keep wearing the brace, maybe it'll heal. So I kept it on. I wore it to work every day. I wore it in our wedding in February. I wore it walking around New Orleans on our honeymoon. I wore it for months, but the leg refused to heal. So the doctor performed another bone graft, and warned me that if he ever operated on my leg again it would be to remove it. Two cautious years later, four and a half years after the accident, he declared it healed but warned me to avoid any activity which might endanger it. I told him not to worry.

Now it was eight years later. I was tired of being cautious, and I guess I didn't really think I would break it again.

"OK, guys, let's go." I looked up to see our jump master smiling as if to say, "It's not going to be as bad as you think; you'll make it." His smile calmed me some. But one memory still had me worried. Back when I was on crutches and people would ask me what had happened, I grew so tired of giving the same answer to the same question that I began to lie. One of my fictitious accounts was that I had broken my leg skydiving. As I walked toward the plane, pulling on my helmet, I thought about how lies can become self-fulfilling prophecies.

When we arrived at the plane, the jump master said, "All right, who's first? Last one in the plane will be the first to jump."

"I'll jump first," I said quickly. If anyone wanted to interpret my desire to go first as heroic, I wouldn't deny it. But I knew the real reason: if I had to watch others jump before me I might become so terrified that I wouldn't be able to do it.

The pilot, then the jump master climbed in through the three-by-five foot door under the right wing. Glen followed and crawled into position behind the jump master. Kula was next. Then I climbed in and sat between the pilot and the door, facing the rear of the tiny cockpit and the fear-whitened faces of my two comrades. When the pilot began to taxi down the runway, the jump master reached across me, pulled the door closed and secured it with a latch at the bottom.

As the small plane struggled in rising spirals toward our jump point at 2,800 feet, I watched the receding earth with mixed feelings. I was so awed by what I was seeing that I could forget my anxiety for seconds at a time. The sun had already set for those people still on the ground. But since we were extend-

SOMETIMES YOU JUST HAVE TO STAND NAKED

ing our horizons the higher we climbed, we were treated to a second sunset: brilliant reds and yellows contrasting with the darkening blanket of misted green that covered the hills and valleys below.

There was little conversation on the way up. The jump master and I exchanged a few words, but I was having increasing difficulty making sense of anything, as if I was floating further away from reality the higher we rose.

Suddenly the jump master reached across me and unlatched the door. It flew up and open, pressed tightly against the bottom of the wing by the force of the wind. My heart was thudding.

Then he looked at me and said, "Sit in the door." This was the first of the three exit commands.

I handed him my bunched-up static line, one end of which was attached to my main parachute sleeve and the other to a ring in the floor of the plane. Then, drawing on my almost depleted reserve of courage, I began turning toward the open door. As I turned, still sitting, I grasped the side of the doorway with my right hand, lowered both feet out of the plane and placed my left foot on a narrow piece of steel located about a foot below the doorway. Then I reached out with my left hand and grabbed the strut which ran from the middle of the wing to a point about two feet in front of the door.

"Out on the strut!" The second command. Though it took a second for the message to penetrate my dizzying consciousness, once it registered I responded almost automatically. Tightening my left-hand grip on the strut, I released my hold on the doorway and simultaneously pushed myself out with my left foot, pulled myself forward with my left hand, and grabbed blindly for the strut with my right. Though my grab was accurate, my muscles were rubbery and nearly useless in the eighty-mile-an-hour wind, and I slumped. But with fear and determination motivating me, I pushed and pulled myself up and forward until my head and shoulders were extended over the strut. I was looking down at barns the size of matchboxes and cows the size of small black ants.

As I clutched the strut, waiting for the final command, I noticed a new feeling beginning to develop. I was no longer concerned about peer pressure, masculinity, my leg. What I was doing had become totally personal. It was a test, one I had set for myself, and one which, if I passed it, would surely be a milestone in my life.

At the same time, I was more frightened than I had been at any other time in my life. I was so frightened that I said an act of contrition, apologized to Suzi, Bridget, Matt and Jude for my recklessness and irresponsibility, told them I loved them, recalled the value of my life insurance, and actually said to myself: I don't care if I die!

"Jump!"   *(to be continued)*

☙   ☙   ☙

Ed: Ahem.

Me: . . . .

Ed: Hey!

CHAPTER 8   THE CONDITIONS OF A SOLITARY BIRD   109

Me:	Uh? Oh . . . hi, Ed.
Ed:	Are you all right? You don't look so good.
Me:	I feel rotten. Look at my hands; they're shaking! I'm having an anxiety attack! Writing that story makes me feel like I'm there all over again.
Ed:	You'd better take a break, then come back and finish it.
Me:	I'll take the break. But I'm not going to finish it tonight. I'll come back to it again in a week or two.
Ed:	You can't be serious!
Me:	Why not?
Ed:	You can't stop now! You're right at the climax. Anybody who has read this far will kill you if you stop here. That's the cheapest trick you can pull.
Me:	Ed, I *can't* write any more on it tonight. I'm afraid I'll mess it up.
Ed:	Let me finish it for you then.
Me:	You? No way. You keep your hands off my story.
Ed:	My, aren't we uppity? It's not like it's some great literary masterpiece.
Me:	It may not be great, but it's mine.
Ed:	Well, do what you want. Your readers aren't going to like it, though.
Me:	Oh, they'll get over it. They're used to it. Besides, deferred pleasure is more fun.
Ed:	Cute.

MORE OR LESS

The more you write, the more you look for ways to say as much as possible with as few words as possible. And that's exactly as it should be. The best writers are the ones who say the most with the fewest words. Not all shortcuts are effective, though; some only seem to give you more for less.

Three *effective* shortcuts are specific details, precise examples and accurate analogies. Because they give readers concrete images to focus on, they are able to show much in a few words. Two *ineffective* shortcuts are abstractions and generalizations. Because they don't give readers concrete images, they actually say less than they seem to. One good picture is worth a thousand abstractions and generalizations. More or less.

ABSTRACTIONS

An abstraction is a word that means different things to different people. Some of the more common abstractions are "love," "fun," "nice," "truth," "security," "beautiful," "wonderful," "patriotism," "thrilling," "exciting," "happiness," "sadness," "boring." Any word that describes or explains something vaguely rather than specifically is an abstraction. Because it doesn't show the readers exactly what you mean, it leaves them free to think what they want. Thus abstractions work against real communication rather than for it.

If I say "She looked sad," I'm giving you a picture, but it's abstract; there are many ways to look sad. I would be more effective if I gave you specific details: "Her chin quivered and her eyes began to tear." Another way to say it more specifically than with an abstraction is with an analogy: "She looked as sad as a rainy Easter."

Obviously there are more words in my substitutes than there are in "She looked sad." But they're necessary for a clear picture. And they show more in fewer words than anything else I might try to use to make the picture as clear, such as more abstractions. The same thing is true in the next examples and in most instances in which there's a choice between being abstract or being clear.

If I say "His father punished him," I'm giving you a picture and I'm only using a few words. But, again, the picture is abstract. It would be much clearer with an analogy or with specific details: "The young father jerked the boy off his feet and slapped his bottom viciously." A picture that falls between those two in clarity is "His father spanked him."

The following brief scene from John Steinbeck's story, "The Chrysanthemums," shows the confusion that abstractions such as "nice," "strong" and "happy" can cause. It also shows how to clear up the confusion with an analogy.

Henry stopped short and looked at her. "Why—why, Elisa. You look so nice!"

"Nice? You think I look nice? What do you mean by 'nice'?"

Henry blundered on. "I don't know. I mean you look different, strong and happy."

"I am strong? Yes, strong. What do you mean 'strong'?"

He looked bewildered. "You're playing some kind of a game," he said helplessly. "It's a kind of a play. You look strong enough to break a calf over your knee, happy enough to eat it like a watermelon."

The trouble with abstractions is that the readers can't see, hear, smell, taste or feel them. I can't see "beautiful" trees; I can see them if you *show* me that they're beautiful. I can't see a "pretty" girl; I can if you give me specific details . . . or if you give me an analogy: ". . . her body was like a clear mountain river of skin and muscle flowing over rocks of bone and hidden nerves."

GENERALIZATIONS

Generalizations, like abstractions, seem to say much but actually say little. "Boys are more aggressive than girls." "She is my best friend; I can always count on her." "I worked diligently but still couldn't meet the deadline."

Each of those statements attempts to cram a great deal of information into a few words. But each fails to communicate anything specific. To make my meaning clear and convincing, I need to either replace the statements with details, analogies or examples, or add details, analogies or examples to the statements.

If I say "It was a beautiful sunset," what have I communicated? About all you know is that there was a visible sunset and that, in my opinion, it was beautiful, whatever that means. *You* don't know whether it was beautiful or not because you can't see it. A beautiful sunset to me might be the one I saw a few days ago: the sun was glowing royal red; some of the clouds were billowy, some stringy, some were white, some snow-cloud gray; the sky ranged from hazy blue to watercolor violet. A beautiful sunset to you might be one that takes place in early summer in a clear sky. So, if I want you to forget your definition of a beautiful sunset for a moment and think about mine, I'm going to have to give you some specific details.

Often, generalizations not only don't clarify, they confuse. "Riding a horse is fun." "Going to school is boring." "She's a wonderful person." "I love you." On the surface, each of those statements seems to say something clear. Notice, though, that each leaves unanswered questions. How is riding a horse fun? Why is school boring? How is she wonderful? How (or why) do you love me? The answers to such questions can be provided effectively and briefly only with examples, details or analogies.

There are times, of course, when generalizations are necessary and adequate. They are useful for summarizing or commenting on something that's either going to be shown or has already been shown. And they are handy for presenting minor information. When you're presenting something important, though, be specific.

NICE TREE

Most of us pass through life noticing only the surface of things, people, experiences. We see something and label it "pretty," we hear something and call it "nice," we feel something and describe it as "pleasant." We do this because it's easier than peeling back and looking below the surface. But what's easy is seldom what's most interesting. What *is* interesting is to explore our sensations, experiences, feelings . . . to notice all the details we can.

The result will be a deeper awareness and appreciation of life. The more used we become to noticing details, the more we'll notice them automatically. Say, for example, I don't normally notice much about trees. If I remind myself to notice details of size, bark texture, color, leaf size and shape, and the variety of insect and animal life in, around and supported by the tree, before long I'll notice those details without having to remind myself to do it. I'll be more aware. My senses note most of these details anyway, but my brain has developed the lazy habit of lumping them together under one generalization: nice tree.

This "lumping" tendency occurs in our writing, too, causing us to be abstract and general rather than detailed. It's easier. Right? But, again, what's easy is not necessarily what's interesting. What *is* interesting is writing that's specific . . . writing that shows and says as much as is necessary with as few words as possible.

Even more important than being interesting is being understood. And if I can describe and explain my experiences and feelings specifically, rather than generalizing about them, I will not only be understood, I might even understand myself.

COOL BREEZE

The statement "Sometimes students have more sense than their professors" is a generalization. An example would make it concrete. Here's one:

> An old prospector is crawling through the desert, nearly dead from thirst, and miles from the nearest source of water.
>
> A student walks up carrying a bunch of grapes. The old prospector is amazed to see someone way out there, in good health, with no water, nothing but grapes. So he asks the student, "Whatcha doin' way out here with just them grapes?"
>
> The student, sucking on a grape, answers, "Whenever I'm thirsty or hungry I just eat a few," and he continues on his way.
>
> The prospector, watching the student fade in the distance, wishes he'd thought about grapes.
>
> A few minutes later, along comes a professor, carrying a car door. The parched prospector is even more amazed by this than he was by the student with the grapes. So he asks, "Whatcha doin' with that there car door, fella?"
>
> Without slowing his pace, the professor rolls down the window, sticks his head through and says: "When I become too hot while walking across the desert, I simply roll down this window and cool myself in the breeze."

   Ž Ž Ž

SUGGESTED PUBLIC WRITING #4

If you don't already have something you care to write about, try this. Recreate the funniest (or most embarrassing, most exciting, most frightening, most painful, most something) experience you've had which also changed you somehow or from which you learned something. Recount the experience in as much detail as necessary for the readers to feel what you felt; include dialogue and descriptions of the place and the people. Show the readers what happened and its effect on you.

Purpose. Depending on the experience you decide to write about, your purpose could be to entertain your readers, to give them something to relate to, to give them something to think about, or all three, or something else. The more you try to accomplish with a writing, the more interesting it's likely to be.

Audience. You could recreate your experience for people who would enjoy or relate to it and/or for people you think would somehow benefit from hearing about it. Your decision about audience, of course, has to be coordinated with your decision about purpose.

Form. Don't say any more than you have to about what led up to and followed the experience. Try beginning at some point within the experience, filling in any necessary background information at convenient points along the way.

Also, don't tell your audience ahead of time what to expect. For example, don't say something like, "The funniest thing that ever happened to me was. . . ." Instead, try beginning with dialogue, thoughts or description of the place or people.

⚭ ⚭ ⚭

ED'S ALTERNATE

Well, that's another one of those cause-effect writings that "Me" is so fond of. How about something completely different? So far, I've given you suggestions involving definition and examples, cause-effect and process analysis and comparison and contrast. This time, see what you can do with classification and/or division. Classification is a type of analysis which sorts things into classes, categories, types. Division is a type of analysis which divides something into its parts.

Classification suggestions: types of people, cars, vacations, schools, clothes, careers. Sample thesis: A baby-sitter needs to know how to cope with all kinds of children. (Then give the characteristics of each major type.)

Another: Deciding on a college or university is difficult. (Then give the advantages and disadvantages of going to a small college, a medium-size college or university or a large university; or of going to college near home or away from home; or of going to a public university or a private or religious one.)

Division suggestions: Review a movie, TV show, book or record by evaluating each of its parts. Sample thesis: Grateful Dead's new album, though not perfect, is well worth the money. (Then evaluate the quality of music and lyrics of several of the songs.) Another: *Apocalypse Now* is one of the best movies I've ever seen. (Then evaluate various aspects of the movie: acting, direction, script, music.)

    💥 💥 💥

Tip #19

Eliminate the word "get" and all of its forms from your writing vocabulary (except when you need it to sound natural, as in dialogue). It is usually an inexact substitute for words that would say what you mean precisely. Besides, it's overused and misused to the point of meaninglessness: get paid . . . how many did you get . . . get busy . . . get drunk . . . don't get upset . . . I got a new car . . . I got married . . . I've got fifteen kids. Try "getting" along without the word except in those rare situations in which it is accurate and no other word will do. I've used the word quite a bit so far in this book, but I dare you to catch me using it again.

    💥 💥 💥

Tip #20

Indefinite subjects such as "student," "parent," "person," "one," "anyone," "someone," "anybody," "somebody" and "nobody" require singular pronouns. For example, "Anyone who wants to drink has to bring *their* own bottle" is ungrammatical; "anyone" is singular, "their" is plural. If the party is for men only, the sentence should be "Anyone who wants to drink has to bring *his* own bottle." If it's for women only, the sentence should be "Anyone who wants to drink has to bring *her* own bottle." However, the party will probably be for both men and women—then what?

Until recently, masculine pronouns (he, him, his) were always used to refer to indefinite subjects; it was understood that "he" might be a man or woman. But many people feel uncomfortable calling what might be a woman "he." Now the most acceptable solution is to use a combination of masculine and feminine pronouns: "Anyone who wants to drink has to bring *his or her* own bottle."

Another alternative that's trying to make its way into general acceptance is "s/he." Try it and see if you like it.

The best solution I've found, though, is to use an indefinite subject that requires a *plural* pronoun, such as "students," "people" or "those," whenever possible. For example: "Those who want to drink have to bring *their* own bottles."

♟ ♟ ♟

Tip #21

When you're describing something like color, shape, height, weight, width, even feelings, it's usually not necessary to mention the word "shape," "color," "feeling" or whatever. "My house is a red color." What else could red be but a color? Try "My house is red."

The same is true of statements like "I had an embarrassed feeling" or "I was feeling embarrassed." What else could embarrassed be but a feeling? In either case, "I was embarrassed" would do.

In other words, if a word's definition includes the general class of which the word is a member, to use both the word and its class word is redundant. For example, embarrassed is defined as a self-conscious feeling. Thus, to say "I had an embarrassed feeling" is the same as saying "I had a self-conscious feeling feeling."

♟ ♟ ♟

VOCABULARY EXERCISE #8

Find ten words that describe types of laughter or ways to laugh (chuckle) and ten words that describe types of crying or ways to cry (sob). Then pick the seven you're most likely to use, define them precisely and use them in imaginative sentences. Do the usual word a day and use the word-definition-sentence format.

The conditions of a solitary bird are five:
The first, that it flies to the highest point;
the second, that it does not suffer for company,
     not even of its own kind;
the third, that it aims its beak to the skies;
the fourth, that it does not have a definite color;
the fifth, that it sings very softly.

San Juan de la Cruz

CHAPTER 9

the good humor man meets mr. hyde

Ice Cream Man
Greg Hennessee

Cecil Horn was tall and thin with high cheekbones, a Roman nose, and thin wavy hair sloping off a high forehead. He was generally thought of as strange by his fellow high school students due to his unusual mannerisms and the fact that he played flute in the band.

Cecil had a ridiculous sense of humor that was infectious yet some-times barely tolerable. He also had what some people call the gift of gab. He could argue anyone down.

He was also probably the cheapest guy I ever met. He was always doing things like making calls from phone booths and then telling the operator he lost his dime in the phone so he'd get a refund.

He was a serious and motivated student, though. He planned on becoming a doctor, and, with his shrewdness and determination, I had faith in him.

I met Cecil through my sister Suzanne, whom he once dated. I didn't start hanging around with him much until the summer of '73. I had just gotten out of high school for the summer and was working at my father's business equipment store, painting the building and doing odd jobs. Cecil came over to my house, having just completed his first year of college, bursting with wild stories and crazy ideas, as full of crap as ever. He'd gotten a job for the summer, driving an ice cream truck around and selling ice cream to little kids. When he told me this I cracked up. He had always managed to get these really strange jobs; while he was in college he worked in a laboratory with diseased rats. But the idea of Cecil as an ice cream man seemed so ridiculous it made me laugh.

One Saturday afternoon when I wasn't working, he drove up in his ice cream truck and asked me if I wanted to ride around with him while he sold his goods. Having nothing better to do, I took him up on it.

The truck was pretty old, an early sixties model of some sort. The cab was painted red. A tomblike white freezer sat on the back, decorated with drawings of ice cream bars like you would see on a drive-in screen during intermission. Above the freezer loomed a wooden board, hand painted with the various prices. It was gaudy enough to be in a carnival.

As we flew down the highway we had to talk louder than normal because the truck was noisy and we both had our windows down. Cecil was wearing a striped tank top and aviator sunglasses that hung on that noble nose like a mountain climber on a peak. His frizzled chestnut hair whipped around in the circulating air as he discussed the boredom of his job.

"This truck doesn't have a radio in it so I have to do something to pass the time. Sometimes I just drive real fast and do crazy things."

We approached an old car creeping down the road. An old man sat at the wheel with his wife next to him. Both seemed oblivious to the world.

Cecil floored the accelerator and began to pass them. A sinister look appeared on his face.

Cecil was the kind of person whose peculiar madness ("inspired insanity" Phoebe Snow once called it) was likely to infect whomever happened to be around him. In this case it was me. Like him, I suddenly felt an urgent desire to freak out the old couple next to us.

As we drove alongside them I reached down and turned up the volume on the truck's music box as loud as it would go, then switched it on. A children's nursery rhyme blared out at a highly distorted level from the speakers on the roof as we passed them doing about seventy. I still laugh when I think how shocked that couple must have been to suddenly see this insidious looking ice cream truck come screaming out of nowhere with children's music blasting and two maniacs in the front laughing crazily. Things like this happened all day.

The wheels of the truck squealed like banshees as Cecil roared around the sharp curves of old country roads, pushing the clumsy vehicle to its limit. I was slightly unnerved at first but soon adapted and found myself laughing along with the driver. He seemed to revel in his insanity.

We drove through the small town of Lewisport heading for Hawesville, where we were to make the rounds selling the icy confections to whomever responded to the electronic music.

I began to think about Cecil in relation to his customers, most of whom must have been small children. The stereotype of an ice cream man is someone nice and kind and good and dedicated to his job, someone who would brave bad weather to deliver his goods, always with a smile and a good word. He is an important facet of the summer months, a signpost of good weather after the hard winter. I had to laugh when I thought of the contrast between this childish ideal and Cecil.

When we reached Hawesville we found what seemed like a suitable neighborhood. Cecil turned on the music and crept down a long dirt road. But when I saw some of the houses bordering it I began to wish we'd never entered the area. It looked like crackerland. I was even more unnerved when some of the people appeared: rough-looking men in dirty T-shirts and John Deere hats, pot-bellied and staring from fly-specked screen doors; haggard-looking women in old dresses scowling at us as their dirty kids jumped and screamed, pleading for money to buy ice cream.

Cecil stopped the truck in front of one of the shacks as a small herd of snotty-nosed kids came bounding toward us, panting with joyful anticipation.

They began climbing over the motionless vehicle like drowning men on a lifeboat, each clutching a few soiled coins. Cecil stood on the platform and commenced taking their money and handing them the desired bars, smiling all the while as he talked to them in a pleasant voice and fished their change out of the white apron which hung loosely over his shorts.

I was sitting in the cab with the window down, trying to mind my own business, when I noticed what I supposed was one of the kid's fathers sauntering up to the truck. He was a grubby-looking heavyset man with dark greasy hair and an oily shirt who mumbled incoherently in a deep voice. As I gazed out the back window I noticed that he and Cecil seemed to be arguing about something.

I sat listening to their voices. Things didn't sound too good. I picked up a few words here and there. The guy was obviously oiled. He slurred his speech all over the place. Cecil was trying to talk to him rationally. He was using a nasally schoolmarmish voice I'd heard him use before when he was confronted with people that he thought were irrational.

As the argument became more audible, I grew a little scared. I knew any minute a fight was going to break out, resulting in God knew what. Probably Cecil getting his bony body pounded into the ground and myself running through the woods being chased by bloodhounds or something. I wanted to get out of there.

Finally, the argument ceased and Cecil climbed back into the truck, unharmed and frowning.

"What happened out there? I thought you were going to get into a fight with that guy. What'd you do, shortchange his kid?"

Cecil just kept frowning and shut the door. "Naw . . . the stupid drunk wanted to buy my truck."

We drove through a few more neighborhoods, this time avoiding anyone who even remotely resembled a hostile parent. Before long, Cecil regained his smile.

I bought an ice cream sandwich from him. I gave him two quarters, which was all the change I had with me, but he stiffly refused to give me my change. I laughed it off as one of his pranks at first, but soon realized he was serious. He was purposely being a creep.

I was a little ticked off at this but let it flow and acted as if it didn't bother me. Then the next time we stopped and he got out for a sale I reached into his change bag, which was lying on the front seat, and got my change. I grinned with the satisfaction of revenge.

As we wheeled down a gravel road we came upon an area which might have been considered Hawesville's slum district. The shacks surrounding the area were considerably worse than the ones we'd previously seen. Mostly black kids were playing in the yards.

Cruising along, amid stares from both sides, we came upon a fork in the road with two dusty driveways leading off to a couple of houses which were partially obscured by a field of tall grass. We almost turned down one of the roads until we noticed that they led nowhere, so we stopped and backed up. Suddenly a grotesque sight appeared before us. An old lady was guiding an idiot along the shoulder of one of the roads to the street we'd just left. The idiot was huge and obese with a short burr haircut, making his head resemble a cantaloupe with five o'clock shadow. He turned and stared at us blankly. Neither of us said anything as Cecil edged the truck forward slowly down the road.

Gazing out at the poverty-infested shacks, I noticed a lanky black kid in cut-offs carrying a watermelon on one shoulder. I shut my eyes in disbelief, thinking of all the bigots I knew who would have loved to have a picture of this. I laughed silently and turned to Cecil, but he was too involved surveying the area for his own purposes.

When he turned on the music, the kids began appearing from everywhere. Most of them were young black kids, full of energy.

We came to a stop in front of one of the shacks and Cecil once more climbed out as I stayed in the cab. Frankly, after that last incident, I would have been perfectly happy to just go home, but Cecil did have his job to do.

The kids were all over the truck. Cecil had the freezer doors open and was handing out bars right and left.

Soon a few older black dudes came up to buy ice cream. And Cecil again managed to get into an argument, this time with a fairly tall, strong-looking, dark-skinned guy in a dark green T-shirt. I listened intently to their conversation. The guy had evidently gotten an ice cream bar and wouldn't pay for it. He was getting mad and began to shout. Cecil argued back. I kept hearing him say, "Well, I can't leave until I get my money." I became a little worried. The guy was really raising a ruckus. "Hey, man, I don't owe you no money! I don't have no ice cream!"

It started getting worse. The guy was becoming violent. "You wanna settle it? Come on down off there, man. Let's duke it out. Come on!"

Cecil stood his ground patiently. "No, I just want the money. If I don't get it, I'll have to put a quarter of my own money in to make up for it." I started to panic. A crowd had gathered to watch the excitement. I knew that at any minute Hawesville's first race riot was going to break out. I had a vision of the mob beating Cecil to death, turning the truck over with me inside, setting it on fire and then marching down the street with torches blazing, singing "We Shall Overcome."

As I sat there sweating, I noticed a middle-aged housewife peering out the screen door of the house we were parked in front of. Suddenly the door slammed back, causing a small shower of rust to rain down, and she ran out looking furious.

"Come here, boy!" she yelled at the guy arguing with Cecil. Then she hurried up to him. "You pay the man what you owe him!"

The angry expression on his face grew angrier. "I don't owe this honky nothin'!"

Cecil patiently interrupted. The nasally voice had returned. "M'am, he took an ice cream bar and didn't pay for it. If he doesn't pay for it, I'll have to myself. I can't leave until I get the money."

Inside the truck I had become frantic. Man, a quarter! He's arguing over a damn quarter. Let's forget it and get out of here! But all I kept hearing was Cecil's seemingly unaffected voice repeating, "I'm sorry, but I can't leave without my money."

The black dude was yelling furiously at Cecil with his fists outstretched boxer-style. "Come on, man; let's duke it out! Come down here and we'll duke it out!"

The woman, who was obviously his mother, grabbed him by the arm. "Stop it! I'll pay the man myself. Get outta my way!" Scowling, she pushed past the frowning son and handed Cecil his quarter, then turned back and resumed reprimanding: "Get in that house! Go on. . . ."

As the crowd dispersed, Cecil climbed into the truck and started the engine. I could still hear the woman loudly complaining as she disappeared into the house, slamming the screen door in another shower of rust.

We were silent for the next few minutes. Cecil was brooding and I was afraid to ask him anything. After that experience, all I could think about anyway was getting out of there.

The brooding came to an abrupt halt as we reached the end of the street and once again confronted the old lady and the idiot, who were still walking a good distance ahead of us, only this time down the center of the street. Suddenly, a maniacal smile flashed on Cecil's face and he growled mock-seriously, "Let's run over this spastic!" I cracked up.

After leaving the Hawesville "ghetto," we found a small country grocery and pulled in. Cecil filled the tank with gas and I went inside and bought some cigars. When I came back out Cecil paid the man and we left.

As we cruised down the highway, I lit one of the cigars and began puffing away. I had the other two in a brown paper bag on the seat. Cecil, out of pure spite, picked up the bag and tossed it out the window. It sailed into oblivion. He grinned and giggled like a hyena on laughing gas.

I was furious. "Hey, dammit! Why'd you do that?" It was futile to ask such questions, though. "Stop the truck! Go back! I want those cigars!" No response. He just grinned and kept on driving. "OK, then, you can pay me back." But I knew he never would.

Once, while hitchhiking through Georgia, Cecil, who loved to hitchhike and did so every chance he got, ran into Lester Maddox in a restaurant and wound up eating dinner with him. Now Cecil, understand, was no fan of Maddox's or anything he stood for, but when the opportunity to meet someone of national prominence presented itself he couldn't resist.

He also couldn't resist coaxing the axhandle-wielding governor into autographing an 8-by-10 black and white glossy of himself as a present for my sister, who hated the man with a passion.

Suzanne had a strange reaction to that picture, which was signed,

"Best wishes to Cecil's girlfriend, Suzanne. Lester Maddox." At first she was irritated but soon she was laughing along with the rest of us. Cecil had a knack for being able to annoy you one minute then make you forget he ever annoyed you the next.

After a while, I was laughing and talking, puffing away on my cigar and digging the experience once again. My resentment had disappeared along with that paper bag.

Soon we were driving through another neighborhood. This one seemed better than the last. It looked better at least.

We turned down one street with the music playing and happened upon some kind of street party. A few little black kids waved from the yard of the house where most of the activity was going on and came running as we pulled up. A couple of big shiny Cadillacs were parked in front, jammed between various other vehicles of assorted sizes and colors. Two black guys were sitting in one of the vehicles with the doors open and loud soul music blaring from a tape deck. People stood in the yard drinking beer and laughing. Someone was barbecuing chicken. The smell drifted deliciously through the air. Everyone seemed to be having a great time. There was no hostility here.

One of the little kids, smiling pleasantly, came up and told us that her mother wanted to trade us a piece of chicken for a bar of ice cream. Cecil was delighted. "Sure," he told her. Excited and giggling, she ran back into the house.

A middle-aged white man in a light blue suit was escorting a well-dressed black lady, drink in hand, onto the porch. Young boys yelled to each other from across the street while two old men, suspenders stretched over bulging bellies, laughed loudly, exposing missing teeth. The atmosphere was cool and relaxed. These people were really enjoying themselves.

The little girl showed up with the chicken. Cecil gave her the ice cream and she ran away, exuberant. We got back into the truck and drove down the street, Cecil steering with one hand and munching on the barbecue.

"Ummm. This chicken's fantastic! This is the best barbecue I've ever eaten." Cecil raved on about the chicken. At the end of the street he had to pull over so he could finish it. "Here, have some; it's delicious," he told me as he pulled off a piece. I chewed it slowly. He was right; it was great.

These were the kinds of experiences Cecil dug. He loved talking about them and always made them sound more fantastic than they actually were. Getting that incredible barbecue from those people and seeing what a great time they were having and how they were expressing their total coolness seemed to make up for all the harassment that had gone down that day.

On the way back, Cecil was cutting up, singing songs and making up dirty lyrics as he went along. His obscene imitations delivered in that nasal twang had us both in hysterics.

When we reached Lewisport we drove through a few trailer courts, then headed back to Owensboro. When we arrived he decided to hit the Fifth Street area before he quit for the night. It was starting to get dark and I wasn't particularly thrilled with the idea, Fifth Street being a rather dangerous place for white folks to be at night, especially on a weekend. But Cecil wanted to pick up a little more money before he quit, so on we went.

As we cruised down one of the back streets, Cecil turned on the headlights and peered into the dusk. A small crowd of black kids came bounding toward us, grinning and yelling for us to stop. We stopped and Cecil got out to do his duty.

After selling as much ice cream as the kids would buy, we told them we had to go. Cecil was a little wary. He was selling in one of his co-worker's areas and was afraid of what would happen if he was spotted.

He kept urging, but the kids wouldn't leave. They pleaded to be given a ride, "just a little down the street." Cecil knew it was against the rules but he couldn't persuade them to get off so, frustrated, he agreed to take them.

We began to creep down the street, the kids hanging on, grinning enthusiastically. Suddenly we heard a noise and Cecil slammed on the brakes and jumped out. The kids all hopped off the back and scattered into the darkness.

"Dammit!" yelled Cecil. "One of those kids opened the freezer and ran off with some ice cream." All the kids had vanished, leaving him standing alone in the red glow of the taillights, haggard and disgusted, largely with his own gullibility. It had been a long day.

Not much happened the rest of that summer. Cecil lived way out in Bon Harbour Hills in a creepy-looking old house not far from a graveyard and I didn't make it out there very often.

We went to a few movies and once drove to Evansville to see *Last Tango in Paris* which had just come out and was creating quite a stir. On the way over something broke on the Volkswagen's clutch and we had to pull off the road. Luckily, we stopped right in front of a garage.

Although it was Saturday evening and the garage was closing, we were able to persuade the mechanic to rig up the broken clutch with a wire that would hold until we got back. It was during this incident that Cecil's penny-pinching nature turned from mischievously amusing to cloyingly insipid. I once had admired him for his originality but now it was wearing thin.

When I offered to buy him a Coke he freaked out. "Uh . . . I don't believe we have enough money to buy a Coke," he proclaimed loudly.

I looked at him as if he was insane. "Of course I've got enough money to buy a Coke," I said.

He shook his head emphatically, standing directly behind the mechanic, and stared at me hard as if to say, "Shut up! You don't know what you're getting us into."

I turned away and dropped my change into the Coke machine. Cecil walked over and spoke in a low voice: "I don't want this guy to know how much money we've got!" I couldn't believe him. I'd never seen him behave this way before.

When the mechanic finished, Cecil tried to sound as destitute as possible. "How much do I owe you? I only have a few dollars." They finally settled on five dollars and we left.

We decided to go on to Evansville and made it to the movie only a little late. When it was over, Cecil was so disappointed with it he couldn't stop putting it down. I wanted to stay and see the part we'd missed, and when I refused to leave he almost left without me.

All the way home he complained about the movie. "It was terrible! The worst piece of crap I've ever seen! Nothing was good about it. The acting was terrible. There wasn't even much sex in it; it was the audience that was getting screwed!"

I liked the movie. At the time I thought Cecil knew something about movies, or at least acting, considering he was a Thespian in high school and all, but now I was disillusioned. He didn't give the film a chance.

I started seeing Cecil less frequently toward the end of summer. Then one night he showed up at my house with the news that he'd wrecked his ice cream truck in another town, coming around a rain-slick curve. Ice cream bars had been scattered all over the highway, and people were stopping their cars and getting out and picking them up, while Cecil, in a confused frenzy, stood on the platform screaming, "Stop! Stop! Leave them alone! They're not yours! Stop!" As a result of the accident he lost his job. But he didn't care; he was going to quit anyway.

Not long after that, he went one more semester at U.K., then decided for some reason to go to school in Seattle. He came by around Christmas and told us of his plans. Then on Christmas day he left, in spite of his mother's objections.

Later on that day we received word that he had been involved in a serious accident and was in critical condition. His Volkswagen had been demolished and he was in a coma. He stayed in that coma for months, so long in fact that I began to doubt whether he would ever come to.

When he finally did come out of it and was allowed to go home, my sister and I went to see him. She had already seen him once and told me how remarkably well he'd recovered. I was anxious to see for myself.

When I saw him I was shocked. He looked terrible. He had lost a lot of weight and looked extremely thin and weak. His hair had been cut short and was swept back in front, revealing a receding hairline. His voice even sounded different. It was shaky and higher pitched. Almost everything about him was changed.

Seeing him so totally different, so awfully weak, had a painful effect on me. Suzanne assured me that he just needed time to recover and that in months to come he would gradually return to normal. But I had my doubts.

I visited him several times in the following months but failed to notice any great change in his condition. He did begin to walk again, which was a great improvement since the doctors had doubted he ever would. But what bothered me most was the fact that he hadn't improved mentally. The sense of humor, the crazy wit, everything that made him such a joy to be around was gone, replaced by a cheap imitation of his former self.

I couldn't help but look at him as a totally different person. It was almost as if the old Cecil had been captured by aliens and replaced with a look-alike android with an extreme case of apathy.

I saw less and less of him as time went on. One night his mother called, quite disturbed. Cecil had disappeared, most likely using his favorite form of transportation, hitchhiking. In any case, he was gone and she had no idea where.

In the following weeks she received several phone calls from him on the road. He was reluctant to tell her where he was and where he was headed, but after much investigation she finally found out. He was in California with some friends, staying in a halfway house. She immediately flew out to get him.

I never did find out what really happened out there; the whole thing was so strange. In the months that followed, I completely lost contact with them. No one ever answered the phone at their house.

Sometime before he had run off to California, Cecil had stopped by to see me and things had ended on an unhappy note. We had gotten into an argument over some ridiculous idea he had and he had stared at me sternly with a deranged look on his face and said, "You think I'm crazy, don't you! You think I'm screwed in the head! You think the accident did something to my brain, don't you!" And having worked himself into a frenzy, he tore off down the driveway.

A few years later I was walking across the lobby of the administration building at Brescia College when I passed a familiar gaunt figure going the other way. At first I wasn't sure whether it was him or not, so I turned for a second glance. As I did, he did the same. What's he doing at Brescia? I asked myself. We stared at each other for a split second and then I turned and walked away.

I had thought of going over to speak to him, but decided against it. What could I have said? What could I have said to that person who looked so much like Cecil Horn, yet whom I really didn't know?

In my mind Cecil was dead. He died in a car accident on Christmas morning, 1974, while children unwrapped presents and Yuletide spirits filled the air. He died, taking with him a unique personality and leaving behind an air of sadness and mystery.

It's been a long time now since that day I last saw him. I have no idea where he is or what he's doing. I keep imagining his thin frame by a roadside somewhere, like a crippled scarecrow, eternally hitchhiking to some unknown destination.

Afterthoughts

Normally when we write about ourselves or something in which we were involved, we present ourselves in the best possible perspective . . . emphasizing or exaggerating our "good" qualities and de-emphasizing or making light of the ones we're not so proud of. We present ourselves as we'd like to be viewed by others rather than as we know ourselves to be. This is an understandable tendency, and it can be beneficial to our self-concepts. But it doesn't make for the most effective writing. One quality that does make for effective writing is a willingness to stand naked . . . to show ourselves as we really are (or were). It's effective because the picture that develops is of a whole person, not just a one-sided ideal. Readers can relate to real people; they can only fantasize about ideals.

Greg is telling a story in which he sees someone else (Cecil) as the main character, but for me Greg (the narrator) is the main character. In the end, he is the one who is most significantly affected by what happens. And because he comes across as a real person, complete with failings, I can relate to him.

❀   ❀   ❀

"Ice Cream Man" is, to me, partly a story about a friendship gone sour, something most of us can relate to. All personalities are a mixture of positive and negative qualities. We remain friends with some people in spite of those elements of their personalities that we don't particularly like. But with others, for some reason the negative qualities become more noticeable and irritating, and the friendship ends. We feel they have changed, though of course few undergo Jeckyl-Hyde transformations to the extent that Cecil does.

We are unduly impressed with some people the first few times we're with them. We can see little or nothing about them not to like. This is especially true in male-female relationships. How many times have you fallen in love with someone who seemed perfect, ideal, only to be disillusioned as you came to see the real person. Jeckyl has become Hyde. Usually in those cases it's not the person who has changed, just your view of the person.

Well, that's some of what Greg's story does for me. What does reading it make *you* think about?

❀   ❀   ❀

EXERCISE

I've put "Ice Cream Man" here as a transition between what I've been talking about and what's coming. And one thing I'd like you to think about before we move on is how much of its effectiveness is due to Greg's adherence to the principles of interesting writing that I've talked about so far.

A. Some things to consider and comment on:

1. His choice of a subject that was meaningful, that he cared about, and that he was qualified by experience to write about;
2. His apparent willingness to give enough time and thought to planning, writing and rewriting;

3. His willingness to give you enough information so you could understand the situation (thoroughness);
4. His liberal use of interesting details, examples and analogies;
5. His willingness to stand naked.

B. Comment also on:

1. The "naturalness" of his narrative voice;
2. The general clarity of his vocabulary;
3. The effectiveness of his dialogue;
4. The effectiveness of his form, including the beginning and ending.

C. Finally, what could he do to make it more effective?

1. Are there places when his vocabulary could be more precise? (Notice
how often he uses a form of "get".)
2. Are there places where he could have said what he was saying with
fewer words?
3. Is there anything that needed more details or explanation?
4. Anything else?

SOMETIMES-YOU-JUST-HAVE-TO-STAND-NAKED SURPRISE. Take a Writing Exercise, Vocabulary Exercise, and Style Self-Analysis vacation. That's
all for this chapter.

One has not only an ability to
perceive the world but an ability
to alter his perception of it;
or, more simply, one can change
things by the manner in which
one looks at them.

Tom Robbins
Even Cowgirls Get the Blues

CHAPTER 10

sao young man: noboory understanos me

psychiatrist: maybe it's your vocabulary

from The End of the Road
John Barth

THE DANCE OF SEX: IF ONE HAD NO OTHER REASON FOR CHOOSING TO SUBSCRIBE to Freud, what could be more charming than to believe that the whole vaudeville of the world, the entire dizzy circus of history, is but a fancy mating dance? That dictators burn Jews and businessmen vote Republican, that helmsmen steer ships and ladies play bridge, that girls study grammar and boys engineering all at the behest of the Absolute Genital? When the synthesizing mood is upon one, what is more soothing than to assert that this one simple yen of mankind, poor little coitus, alone gives rise to cities and monasteries, paragraphs and poems, foot races and battle tactics, metaphysics and hydroponics, trade unions and universities? Who would not delight in telling some extragalactic tourist, "On our planet, sir, males and females copulate. Moreover, they enjoy copulating. But for various reasons they cannot do this whenever, wherever, and with whomever they choose. Hence all this running around that you observe. Hence the world"? A therapeutic notion!

Before you proceed any further into this chapter, go back and read that opening paragraph again. If you aren't certain of the meaning of any of the key words, look them up first. Go on. I'll wait here. (. . . . .

. . . .) Finished? Good.

I wanted you to read that excerpt carefully because I think it's an interesting example of effective use of the language. In one paragraph, Barth has summarized and illustrated a basic Freudian principle, and he's done it clearly, humorously and imaginatively.

When I read something that precisely worded, I'm comfortable. I feel I'm in safe hands . . . the hands of a writer who knows exactly what he's talking about and exactly how to communicate it. Barth uses words so accurately I can almost hear them ping.

Though writing like Barth's is precise, it is also frustrating for readers who are not familiar with the key words. Writers should, of course, adjust their vocabularies to their audiences. But they must also do justice to their subjects and themselves. Those conflicting demands will sometimes cause a writer to use words with which the readers may not be immediately familiar. A conscientious reader will accept the necessity of those words, look them up, and ultimately be grateful for their precision.

Here's another excerpt from *The End of the Road.* The narrator, by the way, is a grammar teacher. (And an "Ed" if I've ever seen one.)

from The End of the Road
John Barth

By this time I was involved enough in teaching so that my moods more and more often had their origin in the classroom. On this particular day, the last Friday in September, I felt acute, tuned-up, razor-sharp, simply because in my grammar class that morning I'd explained the rules governing the case forms of English pronouns: it gives a man a great sense of lucidity and well-being, if not downright formidability, to be able not only to say, but to understand perfectly, that predicate complements of infinitives of copulative verbs without expressed subjects go into the nominative case, whereas predicate complements of infinitives of copulative verbs *with* expressed subjects go into the objective case. I made this observation to my assemblage of young scholars and concluded triumphantly, "I was thought to be *he,* but I thought John to be *him!* Questions?"

"Aw, look," protested a troublesome fellow—in the back of the room, of course—whom I'd early decided to flunk if possible for his impertinence, "which came first, the language or the grammar books?"

"What's on your mind, Blakesley?" I demanded, refusing to play his game.

"Well, it stands to reason people talked before they wrote grammar books, and all the books did was tell how people were talking. For instance, when my roommate makes a phone call I ask him, 'Who were you talking to?' Everybody in this class would say, 'Who were you talking to?' I'll bet ninety-nine per cent of the people of America would say, 'Who were you talking to?' Nobody's going to say, 'To whom were you just now talking?' I'll bet even you wouldn't say it. It sounds queer, don't it?" The class snickered. "Now this is supposed to be a democracy, so if nobody but a few profs ever say, 'To whom were you just now speaking?,' why go on pretending we're all out of step but you? Why not change the rules?"

A Joe Morgan type, this lad: paths should be laid where people walk. I hated his guts.

"Mr. Blakesley, I suppose you eat your fried chicken with your fingers?"

"What? Sure I do. Don't you?"

The class tittered, engrossed in the duel, but as of this last rather flat sally they were not so unreservedly allied with him as before.

"And your bacon at breakfast? Fingers or fork, Mr. Blakesley?"

"Fingers," he said defiantly. "Sure, that's right, fingers were invented before forks, just like English was invented before grammar books."

"But not *your* fingers, as the saying goes," I smiled coolly, "and not your English—God knows!" The class was with me all the way: prescriptive grammar was victorious.

"The point is," I concluded to the class in general, "that if we were still savages, Mr. Blakesley would be free to eat like a swine without breaking any rules, because there'd be no rules to break, and he could say, 'It sounds queer, don't it?' to his heart's content without being recognized as illiterate, because literacy—the grammar rules—wouldn't have been invented. But once a set of rules for etiquette or grammar is established and generally accepted as the norm—meaning the ideal, not the average—then one is free to break them only if he's willing to be generally regarded as a savage or an illiterate. No matter how dogmatic or unreasonable the rules might be, they're the convention. And in the case of language there's still another reason for going along with even the silliest rules. Mr. Blakesley, what does the word *horse* refer to?"

Mr. Blakesley was sullen, but he replied, "The animal. Four-legged animal."

"*Equus caballus,*" I agreed: "a solid-hoofed, herbivorous mammal. And what does the algebraic symbol *x* stand for?"

"*x*? Anything. It's an unknown."

"Good. Then the symbol *x* can represent anything we want it to represent, as long as it always represents the same thing in a given equation. But *horse* is just a symbol too—a noise that we make in our throats or some scratches on the blackboard. And theoretically we could make it stand for anything we wanted to also, couldn't we? I mean, if you and I agreed that just between ourselves the word *horse* would mean *grammar book,* then we could say, 'Open your horse to page twenty,' or 'Did you bring your horse to class with you today?' And we two would know what we meant, wouldn't we?"

"Sure, I guess so." With all his heart Mr. Blakesley didn't want to agree. He sensed that he was somehow trapped, but there was no way out.

"Of course we would. But nobody else would understand us—that's the whole principle of secret codes. Yet there's ultimately no reason why the symbol *horse* shouldn't always refer to grammar book instead of *Equus caballus:* the significances of words are arbitrary conventions, mostly; historical accidents. But it was agreed before you and I had any say in the matter that the word *horse* would refer to *Equus caballus,* and so if we want our sentences to be intelligible to very many people, we have to go along with the convention. We have to say *horse* when we mean *Equus caballus* and *grammar book* when we mean this object here on my desk. You're free to break the rules, but not if you're after intelligibility. If you *do* want intelligibility, then the only way to get 'free' of the rules is to master them so thoroughly that they're second nature to you. That's the paradox: in any kind of complicated society a man is usually free only to the extent that he embraces all the rules of that society. Who's more free in America?" I asked finally. "The man who rebels against all the laws or the man who follows them so automatically that he never even has to think about them?"

This last, to be sure, was a gross equivocation, but I was not out to edify anybody; I was out to rescue prescriptive grammar from the clutches of my impudent Mr. Blakesley, and, if possible, to crucify him in the process.

"But, Mr. Horner," said a worried young man—in the front row, of course—"people are always finding better ways to do things, aren't they? And usually they have to change the rules to make improvements. If nobody rebelled against the rules there'd never be any progress."

I regarded the young man benignly: he would survive any horse manure of mine.

"That's another paradox," I said to him. "Rebels and radicals at all times are people who see that the rules are often arbitrary—always ultimately arbitrary—and who can't abide arbitrary rules. These are the free lovers, the women who smoke cigars, the Greenwich Village characters who don't get haircuts, and all kinds of reformers. But the greatest radical in any society is the man who sees all the arbitrariness of the rules and social conventions, but who has such a great scorn or disregard for the society he lives in that he embraces the whole wagonload of nonsense with a smile. The greatest rebel is the man who wouldn't change society for anything in the world."

Afterthoughts

Whether or not you respect his opinions, I don't think you can help respecting the narrator's style in that excerpt. It's crisp and precise, and it's interesting, in large part because of its music and humor. Speaking of his opinions, what do *you* think of the question, "Should paths be laid where man walks?" Or, "Should man walk where paths have already been laid?" Interesting metaphor, don't you think? Should a person be free to do what he or she wants? Or should a person abide by conventions? (What is a free person?)

If you ask me. . . . (I know you didn't, but I'm going to give you my opinion anyway.) If you ask me, the truth is somewhere between those two extremes. Whether we're talking about living harmoniously or about communicating effectively, if we want to avoid chaos and confusion we need to abide by a few basic, mutually agreeable rules. Actually, one rule is all we need to abide by to live harmoniously: Do unto others as you would have them do unto you. (What a golden rule that is!) And one rule is all we need to abide by to communicate effectively: Be as clear unto others as you would have them be unto you. Within those two rules there is abundant freedom to lay paths wherever one chooses.

Unfortunately, society has become so complex that those two basic rules have had to be interpreted to fit millions of different situations. Thus we have developed the countless laws that govern society and communication, most of them so abstract that they require specialists, lawyers and grammarians, to understand them.

Fortunately, you can't be sent to jail for breaking the rules of grammar. But you will live in a self-imposed prison if you don't abide by that one basic rule: Be clear.

ACCURACY

Another way to say "Be clear" is "Be *accurate.*" And accuracy begins with words. Obviously, the more accurate your words are, the more likely you are to be understood.

But most people don't significantly increase their vocabulary after about the age of twelve. (My estimate.) Yet they grow physically, mentally and emotionally . . . which means that there are depths and nuances of thought and feeling which they experience but which they can't understand clearly or express because they don't know the words that describe them. In a sense, a limited vocabulary confines a person to a limited perception of life. The more life you experience, the more precise words you need to accurately express your thoughts and feelings.

Sad Young Man:	Help me, Doctor.
Psychiatrist:	What's the matter?
Sad Young Man:	I'm sad all the time.
Psychiatrist:	Sad? What do you mean? Doleful? Unhappy? Mournful? Dejected? Rueful? Melancholy? Wistful? Defeated? Futile? Lonely? Despondent? Gloomy? Alienated? Desperate? Blue? Grief stricken? Depressed? Lugubrious?
Sad Young Man:	I don't know. I'm just sad.

Psychiatrist:	Well, I'm sorry. If you can't be any more precise than that, I can't help you.
Sad Young Man:	But, Doctor. . . .
Psychiatrist:	I'm sorry. . . .
Sad Young Man:	Sorry? What do you mean? Pitiful? Wretched? Miserable? Regretful?

Most of us know only a small percentage of the million or so words in our language, and we use even fewer words in our attempts to think and communicate. That would be fine if those few words accurately expressed what we wanted to say. Unfortunately, they don't. So we cheat a little; we use the same few words over and over, trying to make them say things they don't mean. (How many different ways do you use the words "hard," "go," "went," "easy," "nice," "pretty," "hell," "terrible" and "get," for example? And in how many cases would another word express what you mean more precisely?)

I'm not saying we should all be looking up new words with which to impress (and confuse) people. Leave that to the William Buckleys. That's as detrimental to communication as using simple words that don't fit. The idea is to help the readers understand. You can't do that by misleading them with inaccurate words, nor can you do it by confusing them with big, unfamiliar ones.

There are, in the lower realms of your conscious mind, enough accurate words to pull you through most of the communication situations in which you're likely to find yourself. They are words that have slipped in over the years from books, magazines, conversations. You recognize them when you read and hear them, though you probably can't define them. The trick is to move them out of your *recognition* vocabulary and into your *use* vocabulary.

You can accomplish that feat to a high degree by simply forcing yourself to be as precise as you can. You should also develop the habit of using a dictionary when you read and a dictionary and a thesaurus when you write. (Don't shrug that off; you know I'm right.) Use the dictionary to make sure the words mean what you think they mean; use the thesaurus to find possible substitutes . . . not new words that you're unfamiliar with but words you recognize but forget to use.

            ⅋   ⅋   ⅋

VOCABULARY EXERCISE #9

Go back to those excerpts from *The End of the Road.* At the usual rate of one a day, select seven words you recognize and which are close to your vocabulary level but which you aren't quite familiar enough with to use confidently. Look up and write out their definitions. And use each in an imaginative sentence. Use the old word-definition-sentence format.

DENOTATION AND CONNOTATION

There are two sides of accuracy, denotation and connotation. A word's denotation is its current accepted meaning, as listed in a recent dictionary. A word's connotations are its emotional meanings, determined by the associations the word has picked up through years of use.

With many words you'll consider using, you have to think about both denotation and connotation; a word might have the denotation you need but connote something inappropriate. For example, "average," "mediocre" and "normal" have generally the same denotation, but their connotations are different. I don't know about you, but I'd rather be referred to as "normal" or even "average" than "mediocre" because over the years "mediocre" has picked up some negative connotations. For the same reason, most underweight people would rather be referred to as "thin" than "skinny," "skeletal" or "emaciated." And most overweight people would rather be referred to as "full-bodied" than "fat," "pudgy," "rotund" or "obese."

There are several words in those excerpts from *The End of the Road* that Barth obviously chose for what they connote as well as for what they denote. Here's one example: "What could be more charming than to believe that the whole *vaudeville* of the world, the entire dizzy circus of history, is but a fancy mating dance?" In this context, of course, "vaudeville" is a metaphor, implying a comparison between the world (human behavior) and vaudeville (a stage show consisting of mixed specialty acts, including songs, dances, comic skits, acrobatic performances, etc.). That definition in parentheses is the word's current *denotation*. In addition, "vaudeville" *connotes* something humorous; when people who remember vaudeville think about it, they smile. Barth could have said "human behavior" instead of "the whole vaudeville of the world." "Human behavior" is accurate denotatively, but it doesn't connote anything. He could also have said "the whole Broadway of the world" or "the whole Hollywood of the world," but neither of those expressions has the kind of connotation he's looking for to establish this simplified, comic view of human behavior.

"Vaudeville" is an effective word, then, for a number of reasons. As a metaphor, it provokes the reader to think about human behavior in an unusual and interesting perspective: a stage show consisting of mixed specialty acts. And its connotations are appropriate: human behavior is comical when you think about it the way Barth suggests. "Vaudeville" is also effective in this context because it's surprising.

SURPRISE

A word's accuracy of meaning (denotative and connotative) is not the only consideration when you're looking for an effective word. There is also the surprise value of a word or word combination.

In order to keep the readers' interest, it's necessary to hold their attention. A good way to *lose* their attention is to use only those words and phrases which come most quickly to mind. They come quickly because you've heard and used them so often. If your words and phrases are consistently common, familiar, expected, trite, your readers are likely to drift away. On the other hand, if your words and phrases are too unusual, they will be confused and irritated and stop reading. What you need are well-timed verbal surprises to keep snapping your readers back to attention.

There are several examples of surprising words in those excerpts from *The End of the Road.* Here are two: "If one had no other reason for choosing to *subscribe* to Freud, what could be more *charming.* . . ." Most people would have said "believe" or "accept" rather than "subscribe to," and they would have said "satisfying" rather than "charming." ("If one had no other reason for choosing to believe Freud, what could be more satisfying. . . ."—denotatively clear, but dull.) In addition to being surprising, "subscribe" and "charming" put the matter in an interesting new perspective.

As I pointed out back in Chapter 7, this same theory applies to analogies. Clichés are familiar and unsurprising and are therefore ineffective in holding the readers' attention. Original similes and metaphors are surprising and therefore effective.

SOUND

One more consideration in word choice, a final refinement, is sound. Some words sound better in a given situation than others that could be used to express the same concept. And some word combinations sound better. Because they appeal not only to the mind but also to the ear, they help to hold the readers' attention and interest. Even if your readers don't consciously realize that you're playing with the sounds of words, those sounds will register on their subconscious and affect their reactions to what you're saying.

The most common sound categories are alliteration, assonance, consonance, euphony, cacophony and onomatopoeia.

Words *alliterate* when they repeat the same initial sound, the first sound in the words. Thus, "*t*ired *t*oddlers" alliterates, while "*t*ired *ch*ildren" doesn't. "*Autumn auction*" alliterates; "*fall sale*" doesn't. "*Holding hands is heaven*" does; "*locking fingers is fun*" does; "*entwining fingers is exciting*" does; but "*entwining fingers is heaven*" doesn't. From *The End of the Road:* "*paragraphs and poems*" . . . "*whenever, wherever and with whomever.*"

Words are *assonant* when they repeat a vowel sound anywhere in a group of two or more words. "*Hard arch*" is assonant; so are "*dirty word,*" "*slippery hips,*" "*cold nose,*" and "*resplendent elephant.*" From *The End of the Road:* "*fancy mating dance*" . . . "*battle tactics.*" (Notice that it's not the letters themselves that constitute assonance but rather the sounds they produce. One letter can produce several different sounds; different letters can produce the same sound. Thus, "*rotten orange*" is not assonant; "*pretty women*" is.)

Words are *consonant* when they repeat a consonant sound anywhere in a group of two or more words. "*Rattle trap*" is consonant; so are "*lucky duck*" and "*remember my mother.*" From *The End of the Road:* "*fancy mating dance*" . . . "*helmsmen steer ships.*"

One general effect of alliteration, assonance and consonance is to call attention to the phrases in which they occur and make them memorable: hickory dickory dock. If overused, though, the effect is ridiculous. As a general rule, use them to call attention only to important details or ideas.

Phrases and sentences are *euphonious* when they are pleasing to the ear; when they flow smoothly and quietly. They are *cacophonous* when they don't flow smoothly. You might use euphonious phrasing to describe or explain something pleasant, cacophonous phrasing for something unpleasant.

Euphony and cacophony can be achieved by controlling sentence length and variety, too, and sometimes by purposely repeating sentence patterns. If you're describing something intense, a series of short, choppy sentences would be appropriate because they would simulate the rapid heartbeat that normally accompanies an intense experience. Long, smooth, flowing sentences would be appropriate for describing something pleasant. In most writing, a mixture of the two is an effective way to hold the readers' attention. If all or most of your sentences are either short and simple or long and complex, your readers will tire of reading. If you vary your sentences (now a compound, now a simple or two, now a complex, etc.), you in effect keep surprising your readers and therefore keep them awake and interested.

Onomatopoeia, in spite of its puzzling name, is really simple. Words are *onomatopoetic* when they sound like what they describe: "buzz," "chirp," "bang," "snap." "Onomatopoeia" is obviously not one of those words.

Words sound good alone and together for lots more reasons than these. But naming and memorizing them is not what's important. What is important is that you become conscious of the music of words and incorporate that consciousness into your rationale for choosing one word over another.

So ... there is a lot to consider in word choice. But there are priorities. The first and most important consideration is always accuracy ... followed by surprise ... then sound. Whatever you do, don't use a word that sounds good but which doesn't say what you mean as accurately as another word.

⅋ ⅋ ⅋

EXERCISE

Trot back to those excerpts from *The End of the Road*. (1) Find several words that you think are well chosen because their connotations suit what Barth is saying. Explain your choices. (2) Find several words that attracted your attention because you were surprised to run across them in that context. Explain why they are both surprising and appropriate. (3) Find several places where Barth uses sound effectively. Explain the effect.

Now, trot back even further, to one of the student writings or to a segment of "A Solitary Bird" and perform the same analyses: connotation ... surprise ... sound.

Finally, analyze one of your own writings. Find places where your words are effective because of their connotations, their surprise value and their sounds. Then find places where you could be more effective for one or more of the same reasons.

⅋ ⅋ ⅋

Tip #22

Don't say "I feel" or "I feel like" when what you mean is "I think" or "I believe." "Feel" has to do with emotions: I feel good; I felt relief; I feel foolish writing this. It also pertains to sensations: I feel raindrops on my head; I felt her hand sliding across my shoulder. But "feel" doesn't pertain to thought or belief. In the statement "I feel the best thing to do is quit," the speaker isn't talking about an emotion or a sensation but a thought. Thus the speaker should have said, "I think the best thing to do is quit."

⅋ ⅋ ⅋

Tip #23

Don't say "you" when you mean "I" or "me." The statement "Listening to this music makes you think strange thoughts" should read "Listening to this music makes me think strange thoughts." The person who wrote the first of those two sentences was talking about himself, not his readers, so he should have used first person. Though there are exceptions, a good general rule is this: Only use *you* (second person) when you are talking directly to the readers.

       ❀   ❀   ❀

Tip #24

Don't say something "seems" to be true when, as far as you're concerned, it *is* true. In fact, avoid all unnecessary qualifiers, such as "probably," "maybe," "possibly," "in my opinion," "I think," "to me." Sometimes they're necessary, but often they're not. When you say something *seems* to be the case, you sound as if you're not sure of what you're talking about. If you're *not* sure, then by all means say "seems." Otherwise, be definite. Example: "The stench of cigarette smoke seemed to permeate the room" is unnecessarily cautious. What the writer means is "The stench of cigarette smoke permeated the room." The readers need to believe that the writer knows what he or she is talking about. A writer who qualifies unnecessarily doesn't generate much confidence.

       ❀   ❀   ❀

SUGGESTED PUBLIC WRITING #5

If you don't already have a subject you care to write about, consider this: Recreate an experience which involved some sort of a pleasant or unpleasant surprise ... and which changed you somehow or from which you learned something, or which for some other reason is meaningful to you. It can be a big or little surprise; it may have changed you a little or a lot, internally or externally; you may have learned something major or minor; the important thing is that the experience has come to mean something to you. And it's that meaning which you'll be showing to your readers with the example of your experience.

     If at all possible, avoid explaining (telling) how you were changed or what you learned or what it means to you. Instead, try to recreate the experience so that its importance is clear and speaks for itself.

     Also, don't tell your readers ahead of time what to expect. Try to make the surprise as surprising for them as it was for you.

     When you're searching back through your life to see if you have an experience that fits this suggestion, be open to those experiences which more or less began with the surprise rather than ended with it.

       ❀   ❀   ❀

ED'S ALTERNATE

This time see what you can come up with by combining two or more of the rhetorical methods in ways different from those I've already suggested. For example, you could combine process analysis, classification and examples to explain what you've learned about how to catch different types of fish. You could classify the fish into, say, blue gill, bass and crappie; you could explain the steps involved in catching each type (process analysis); and you could use examples from your own experience to make the writing clear and interesting.

Or, you could combine comparison and contrast with definition and examples to explain the relative merits of different social activities (things to do on a night out). Use definition (with examples) to clarify the nature of each activity, and comparison and contrast for evaluating the activities.

You could even make a challenging game of it: put the different rhetorical methods in a hat (example, comparison and contrast, definition, classification, division, cause-effect, process), draw out two or three, and let them guide you in finding a subject and writing about it. Fun, huh?

ONE MORE THING

While taking a break a few minutes ago, I was thinking about what I had said earlier about using surprising words to make writing interesting. And I ended up thinking about what makes *people* interesting. My thoughts are simple and beside the point, but here they are anyway. (It's my chapter.)

People can't be interesting if their stimuli aren't varied and interesting. If their lives are repetitious and boring, they'll be repetitious and boring. It's up to each person to make it otherwise, by seeking out and exposing himself or herself to a variety of influences . . . in life, in books, in music, etc. The more varied and interesting people's intake, the more interesting their output.

Most people I know find a rut in which they're comfortable and stay there. The more interesting people I know, when they see that they're in a rut, step out of it. They try different experiences, different challenges, different authors, different music . . . they change schools, change jobs, change life-styles . . . just to expose themselves to new stimuli and make their lives more interesting.

They take risks. They believe that an interesting life is more important than a secure life. They live on the edge. Good for them.

And what do *I* do? Write the same book . . . over and over and over. . . .

A growing person
needs a
growing vocabulary.

CHAPTER 11

ed's opportunity

Some textbook chapters on wordiness begin with a paragraph in which the author is as wordy as possible. It's a childish attempt to satirize all the student wordiness the author has to deal with. I'm not going to do that, though. My own writing is wordy enough as it is. And nobody is as wordy as those exaggerated examples. Besides, making fun of people for being wordy is like making fun of people for smoking or for being socially inept. They already know they have a problem; they just don't know what to do about it.

I'm just going to try, as much as possible, to give you explanations of what all this business about wordiness is and, also as much as possible, try to explain what you, as an individual unique person in these confusing and wordy modern times, can do about it (your wordiness). I just really can't stand or relate to teachers and instructors and professors of writing who, because of some inflated but mistaken notion of their own superiority, think it's funny or humorous to satirize, ridicule and generally make fun of the way some of their students express themselves in writing. To me, the way I see it, from my point of view, speaking subjectively of course, they just turn off and alienate the very people they think they are helping and aiding with what they have to say about how people should write, ideally, when they write. Besides. . . .

Ed: Stop that. It's not funny.

Me: I know it isn't. It was fun, though, writing without restraints. Like running naked in the sun.

Ed: It may be fun to write but it's tiresome to read.

Me: Uh, I think that was the point, Ed.

WHAT DIFFERENCE DOES IT MAKE?

Once I cut about a quarter of the words from a student's writing. When I handed it back to her she asked, "What difference does it make if I'm wordy as long as the readers understand what I'm saying?"

"The difference," I told her, "is this: If you're wordy, you make the readers work too hard, you waste their time, and you distract them from what's important."

She asked me to explain.

"Well," I said, "when you use unnecessary words, the readers have to *work* to understand what you're saying. The writer is supposed to do the work; the readers are supposed to enjoy themselves and possibly learn something."

"That makes sense," she said.

I continued: "Wading through unnecessary words is a waste of time."

"That's true," she said. "But. . . ."

"Every word you put before your readers demands their attention. If you give them more words than necessary, you stretch their attention thin and distract them from what's important."

"That all makes perfect sense," she said, "but it doesn't solve my problem. How can I get rid of my wordiness?"

"I'm glad you asked," I said.

TWO THINGS TO REMEMBER

The first thing to remember about wordiness is this: When something you're trying to explain is not clear, *more* words won't necessarily help; *accurate* words will.

The second thing to remember is this: The more words you know, the fewer you'll have to use.

A third thing to remember (make that "Three Things to Remember") is this: Most wordiness is caused by uncertainty. You're uncertain either because you don't know your subject well enough to be writing about it, or because you don't know for certain what you want to say or show about it, or because you haven't thought about it enough to figure out what words best explain it. The only solution is to write about what you know from firsthand experience, and to plan, write and edit it carefully.

REPETITION

There are different types of wordiness. The easiest to recognize and eliminate is repetition of words and ideas, saying the same thing twice when once would do. (Like that.)

An early draft of this chapter included the following two sentences: "A student asked me, after I had cut about one fourth of her words, why I thought that was necessary since what she had said was pretty clear. In other words, what difference does it make whether you're wordy as long as the reader can figure out what you're saying?" That's repetitious because both sentences express the same idea. So I cut-and-combined them, saving what I liked best and discarding the rest. In this version of the book, I've cut it even more, and turned the sentence into dialogue.

   ⌘ ⌘ ⌘

EXERCISE

Eliminate unnecessary repetition in the following sentences. Notice that this type of wordiness usually can be eliminated simply by cutting.

1. John hates to write; he can't stand putting his thoughts on paper.
2. Mary loves to dress up and put on her best clothes.
3. It was 6:00 A.M. in the morning.
4. Fill the gas tank with all the gas it can hold.
5. He is a man who knows where he is going.
6. His idea for solving the energy crisis is a good idea.
7. She is the type of person who takes advantage of every interesting opportunity.
8. The color of my car is red.
9. I'm not a wordy person, not by any means.
10. A wordy sentence is one that uses more words than it needs to use to say what it's trying to say.

Now, write two sentences that repeat *words* unnecessarily. Then, write two sentences that repeat *ideas* unnecessarily.

UNNECESSARY INFORMATION

Another relatively easy type of wordiness to recognize and eliminate is unnecessary information. It appears in the forms of over-explaining, over-writing and straying from the point.

Over-explaining is saying more than is necessary to be understood. This usually is caused by the writer underestimating the intelligence of the audience. The readers feel talked-down-to when they read it, as if the writer thinks they are too stupid to understand. The best way to prevent over-explaining is to know your readers and keep them in mind as you write. Tell them what they need to be told in order to understand, and no more. Don't waste their time with information they already know.

Over-writing is being overly detailed, or giving too many words to a minor detail, or including impressive but unnecessary words. In the first two instances it's a problem of balance. In the last one it's showing off (but, ironically, appearing foolish).

Straying from the point is caused by temporarily losing sight of your purpose. If you don't have a clear sense of the point you want to make from the start, you're likely to stray all over the place.

In an earlier draft of this chapter I strayed from the point when I was talking about how things that waste your time are aggravating:

> Someone who wastes your time is stealing that which is most important to you. None of us have enough time to do everything we'd like to do. So we establish priorities. I can't be a husband, father, friend, teacher, reader, writer, bartender, doctor, artist, guru, politician, snake charmer, anthropologist and rear admiral in the U.S. Navy. So I make choices and do as many as I think I can comfortably divide my time among. This leaves little or no time to spare. That's why when someone or something demands more of my time than I think is warranted, I become nervous and resentful.

I knew as I was writing it that all that was beside the point (and over-explaining). But I was curious to see where the thought was going so I kept after it, with the intention of cutting it later. Chase stray rabbits down as many deviant paths as you like; it can be fun and there's no telling what you might discover. But remind yourself as you're doing it to cut it when you're finished.

If you want to avoid straying altogether, plan carefully before you begin to write.

TOO MANY WORDS

The most common type of wordiness and, for some people, the most difficult to correct is the use of two or more words to say what could be said precisely with one. This is a vocabulary problem. The writer doesn't know, or hasn't taken the trouble to find, the most precise word for the job. For example, "I *took a leisurely walk* down the street" could be more precisely stated "I *strolled* down the street."

Another example: "If I continue to look on my hands as the two miracles they are, I'll have no *problem in trying to figure out what* work that is intended for them." The person who wrote that sentence use eight words (italicized) to say what could have been said precisely with two: *difficulty discovering.* Most readers have a lot more confidence in a writer who says "I'll have no difficulty discovering" than in one who says "I'll have no problem in trying to figure out what is. . . ."

Sometimes people use a precise word but, because they're not certain of its strength and true meaning, they tack on one or more words to try to strengthen it. But those extra words have the opposite effect; they weaken and muddy the concept. Tip #16 (page 90) . . . very/really . . . has to do with this. Thus, "She's a pretty girl" is stronger than "She's really a very pretty girl." And stronger than either of those is "She's pretty."

❀ ❀ ❀

EXERCISE

In the following sentences, cut unnecessary words and/or replace fat phrases with precise words.

1. That joke is very ambiguous.
2. He pushed the bucket down under the water.
3. The bright sunset lit up the western part of the sky.
4. This is important stuff; really try to pay attention.
5. When I flipped on the switch and turned the blender on, the top of it blew off and the walls got disgustingly splattered with frozen daiquiri.
6. The tracks extended in the same direction and were the same distance apart at every point.
7. I moved my legs really rapidly in order to get there just as fast as I possibly could.
8. I'm going to go out to the highway and stick out my thumb and get a ride to town.
9. The music at the concert was really good; I moved back and forth from side to side all night long.
10. The person who wrote this book has a very sick sense of humor.

Now, become a wordy person again and write two sentences in which you say something in two or more words that could be said precisely with one. Then write two sentences that include unnecessary adverbs and other verbal clutter.

MAKE EVERY WORD COUNT

When you're finished with a writing, look again at each word, each phrase, each sentence, each paragraph, and ask yourself, "Is it necessary?" If it's not, cut it. Replace fat phrases with precise words. (Sometimes, especially

you know is awkward and unclear, simply cutting a few
..lp.) Make every word count. Overcome the notion that every-
.written is worth reading simply because you wrote it.

..ED?

.., I've been telling you to be detailed and thorough. Now I'm telling
you to not use so many words. In case you're confused by this apparent
contradiction, thoroughness refers to information; wordiness refers to the
words used to communicate that information. Include as much information as is necessary for your readers to understand what you mean, but use
as few words as possible to communicate that information. In other words,
be both thorough and precise.

WRITING EXERCISE _____

Sometimes an effective way to write about something is to write as if you are
someone else. You can do it as a way of making fun of the type of person
you're imitating (ridicule or satire). Or you can do it as an experiment in
looking at the world as someone else perceives it. Or you can do it for some
persuasive purpose, such as arguing against war (or anything) as if you
were a victim of it.

Fiction writers sometimes "become" one of their characters and tell
the story from that character's point of view and in that character's words.
It's a useful way to develop a character because everything he or she says,
and the way he or she says it, shows what kind of person the character is.
The excerpt that follows is from a novel called *The Fan Man*, by William
Kotzwinkle. The character Kotzwinkle created to tell the story is an interesting "hippie" named Horse Badorties. Notice how quickly and well you
know him as a result of what he says and the way he says it.

Directly across from me, man, is the subway window. And since it is
dark in the tunnel and lighted in the subway car, I can see my Horse Badorties
head reflected with hair sticking out in ninety different directions. Weird
looking Horse Badorties. Horse Badorties making demon little ratty face,
crawling eyeballs into corners, wrinkling nose up like rodent, pulling gums
back, sticking teeth out, making slow chewing movements. Freaking myself
out, man, and several other people in the car.

Fanning myself with plastic breezes, making weird faces, what else,
man, is needed? Only one other thing, man, and that is a tremendously deep
and resonant Horse Badorties Tibetan lama bass note which he is now going
to make:

Braaaaaaaaaaaaaauuuuuuuuuuuuuummmmmmmmmmmmmmmmnnnnnnn.

SOMETIMES YOU JUST HAVE TO STAND NAKED

Mothers with their children look at me, man, and then explain to their kiddies that if you don't learn to blow silent farts in church you will turn out like that awful man. But the kids know, man, they know it is better to freely release the energies.

Okay, here's the exercise: Pretend you're someone else, either someone you like, someone you don't like or just someone you think is interesting. This doesn't have to be someone you know; it can be someone you make up to represent a certain type of people. As this person, say things that will clearly show what he or she is like. Your purpose can be to make fun of such people, to show the world as they see it, or to try to right some wrong. Your audience should be the people you most want to be affected by what this person has to say and/or by what you want to show about this person.

One nice thing about this exercise is that it allows you to ignore rules that apply when you're writing as yourself. As this other person, you can be as wordy as you'd like him or her to be, or as ungrammatical or disorganized. Don't forget, though, that you do want this to have a particular effect on your audience. If it's incomprehensible or tiresome, it can hardly be effective.

Here's what one student wrote.

Things Not Seen
Nancy Leffel

I grew up in that house. I mean, I didn't really grow up there, I just dreamed about it, off and on, for years. I could tell you in detail the pattern of the etched glass over the arched windows in the living room. The sun shining through them at midday created prisms of light that reminded me of twinkling stars. Polished walnut banisters curved up to the second floor, where my bedroom waited, bejeweled in layers of pink and white lace. The huge bed was hidden by dozens of soft, billowy pillows, each one beckoning me to sink into bottomless slumber.

A tree house nestled among the branches of an old oak tree in one corner of the back yard. The permanent steps were built to handle many visitors, but, being a recluse, I improvised a gate at the top to secure my aloneness. I would hide there for hours, watching the world from a bird's point of view. How many times I had wished to join a feathered family and fly off on untethered wings.

The one thing missing from my frequent dreams were the occupants of the house. I lived there. And so did my mother and father. It's just that I never saw them. I mean, I felt them, walking through the rooms with me, but I never really saw them.

Yesterday a new Grand Prix with a two-tone green paint job was parked in front of me. Today there is an old navy blue Mustang. I am grateful for the change.

Everything is pretty much on schedule. The maid arrives at eight thirty-five, five minutes late, as usual. The mailman walks up at nine o'clock, rings the bell, and waits for the maid to take the handful of envelopes. A huge silver mailbox hangs beside the big carved doors, but it is never used. At nine fifteen a white car backs out of the driveway, turns east, and drives away. Good, he didn't see me. I pour some coffee from the thermos and turn on the radio. It will be another forty-five minutes before anything else happens.

At ten o'clock the maid opens the big double doors and cleans the outside glass. She skips the top quarter of the doors, which are smudged with dirt from previous neglect. She moves from there to the living room windows, the dining room windows, and a small hard-to-reach window on the end of the porch.

I sit up, stretching my legs and pushing my arms against the top of the car to keep them awake. A young red-faced boy unlocks the car in front of me, glances briefly in my direction, and drives away. Now my car is the only one parked on this side of the street.

At twelve noon I unwrap a sandwich and eat it very slowly. Why do I keep bringing the same old ham and cheese? Must be in a rut. Tomorrow I'll bring cream cheese and olive. The coffee is cold.

At one o'clock, the old lady walks up the street, her short shuffling gait never changing. She stops at the first step to the porch, inspects the windows, then carefully mounts the steps, always climbing with the left leg. She barely touches the bell before the doors open, and a disjointed arm helps her disappear into the house. The doors close behind her as if pushed by a sudden wind.

My cramped restless body urges me to leave early. Nothing has changed. I glance in the mirror, noting the dark circles under the blue eyes. I run a comb through the thick black hair, and pat some powder on the sallow skin. It will probably be another hour before the old lady leaves. Maybe, just today, I'll leave before she does.

But I don't. I'm held to this place as sure as the big old oaks that shadow the yard. I wish I could leave. But I can't, and won't. Not yet.

It's three o'clock. Soon the white car will return. The big walnut doors open and the old lady shuffles out, stumbling over the doorsill. I wait for the doors to close behind her, but they don't. Instead, another woman, perhaps twenty years younger, steps out, and gently helps the older one down the steps. She's not supposed to do that; she always stays in the house. For a moment I turn away, afraid of being seen. But I've been waiting too long for this. I turn back to them. They walk unsteadily, the younger one supporting the older, down the driveway to the main sidewalk. They are talking. The younger woman's black hair is steaked with gray. As they pass my car, she glances at me, and stops.

I should leave, run, hide as fast as I can. Her eyes hold me. Their blueness envelops me, takes me in, cushions me. We have finally met.

The old woman watches us. "Do you know that young woman?" she asks her companion.

The younger woman hesitates, our eyes still locked, then fades away from me. "No, Mother. She just looks like someone I knew a long, long time ago. I was mistaken." They walk arm in arm down the street, and around the corner.

My eyes cling to them until they disappear. Her words echo off the walls of my mind. I squeeze my eyes shut for a moment, then open them as an old beat-up white Chevy pulls into the gravel driveway. I watch as the man climbs the old wooden steps to the porch, careful to avoid the rotting boards. He retrieves the mail from the scratched gray box next to the door, and fumbles for his keys. Unlocking the door, he steps inside, slamming it shut behind him. Pieces of dirt and white paint tumble down silently, covering the doorway like a dusty shroud.

    უ   უ   უ

Afterthoughts

What can you conclude about this woman from what she says and the way she says it? Why does she park in front of this house day after day? What is her relationship to the two women who emerge from the house? Why have all the details of the house changed in the last paragraph? What is the significance of her statement at the end of the second paragraph: "How many times I had wished to join a feathered family and fly off on untethered "wings"? And, in the next paragraph, what is the significance of this statement about her parents (in her dreams about the house): "I mean, I felt them, walking through the rooms with me, but I never really saw them"?

    უ   უ   უ

Tip #25

Don't use present progressive or past progressive tense verbs (e.g., is writing, was writing) when simple present or past tense verbs will do (writes, wrote). The progressive tenses (and other -ing predicates) are less definite and often unnecessarily wordy. For example, "On the north side *is a porch running* across the front" could be more directly and clearly worded: "On the north side *a porch runs* across the front." "Fish *were darting and running* past my legs" should be "Fish *darted and ran* past my legs."

    უ   უ   უ

Tip #26

A strange expression I've noticed lately is "try and do" or "try and help." People seldom try *and* do anything. Normally they try *to* do something. "I'm going to try *and* help her" should be "I'm going to try *to* help her." "I'm going to try *and* see that movie" should be "I'm going to try *to* see that movie." "Try *and* come over later" should be "Try *to* come over later."

    უ   უ   უ

Tip #27

There is no such word as "alot." It's two words: "a lot." "There are *alot* of mistakes in this paper" should be "There are *a lot* of mistakes in this paper." Now that that's clear, try to eliminate "a lot" from your writing. Like "get" and "thing," it's abstract, overused and usually replaceable with a precise word or phrase.

    ❀   ❀   ❀

STYLE SELF-ANALYSIS #4

If necessary, reread the directions on page 50. (I realize that these self-analyses can be a pain, but they're necessary. Writing has to become a conscious activity before it can be fully effective. Anyhow, like many beneficial things in life, if it wasn't difficult it wouldn't be worth doing. Hang in there.)

Sample

Strength   I work hard to find and cut my wordiness.

Weakness   I use "a lot" a lot.

Corrective   Stop being so lazy; find the precise word.

Deadline   Immediately.

Something else I'm doing to make my style more effective   I'm still studying my handbook.

Weakness that's already been corrected   I've stopped writing too-long sentences.

    ❀   ❀   ❀

VOCABULARY EXERCISE #10

List ten adjectives or nouns of two or more syllables that describe different levels or types of happiness (delight, ebullient). Then list ten adjectives or nouns of two or more syllables that describe different levels or types of unhappiness (despair, pessimistic). Then, at the usual rate of a word a day, pick the seven you're most likely to be able to use, define them precisely, and use them in interesting sentences. (Use the word-definition-sentence format.)

    ❀   ❀   ❀

Me: Well, Ed, do you like this chapter?

Ed: I don't know how to tell you this.

Me: What? What's the matter?

Ed: Your chapter on wordiness is *wordy*.

Me: That's a matter of opinion.

Ed: You've repeated words and ideas, you've strayed from the point, you've over-explained, over-written and floated on a fat phrase now and then.

Me: Yeah? Well, it's easy enough to just sit back and criticize. I'd like to see *you* do any better.

Ed: Do you mean it?

Me: Yeah, I mean it.

Ed: Thanks! I've been hoping for an opportunity like this since Chapter 1.

CHAPTER 11 (REVISED)

by *Ed*

If you're wordy, cut it out.

CHAPTER 12

"jump!"

A Solitary Bird, Part V

Terrified by the view below, I jerked my head up. When I did, my helmet banged against the underside of the wing, which made me wonder: Am I too *tall* to be doing this? What about the tail? What's it going to do to my head when I let go of this strut? I had asked about this earlier and our instructor had assured me that no skydiver had ever lost his head to a tail. But, squinting into the wind, my helmet rapping against the wing, I wasn't so sure.

There was one comfort, though: I wouldn't have to pull a real rip cord to open my parachute. I was attached to a static line that would take care of that. But, like an umbilical cord, its function would be short-lived. A few seconds after I let go of the plane, it would pull the sleeve off my parachute and I'd be on my own, half a mile in the sky, either drifting in an open chute, spinning in a Mae West or plummeting in a total malfunction.

When I heard the command to jump, I was supposed to simultaneously release my grip on the strut and lift my left foot off the little steel bar, and immediately "hit a hard arch"—which means I was supposed to fall belly-downward, with my head and legs back, and my arms spread like bird wings. This was necessary so that the main parachute, which was harnessed on my back, could open straight up. If I lost control and fell back-downward (butt first), in what they called the "inverted arch," the parachute would be forced to open under me and slide around my body, which could be disastrous.

Also on letting go of the plane, I was to count to 6,000 by thousands (1,000 . . . 2,000 . . . 3,000 . . . etc.), hitting the hard arch on 1,000 . . . drawing both hands in to my chest on 2,000 . . . grasping and pulling the "dummy" rip cord on 3,000 . . . re-extending both arms on 4,000 . . . checking to see if the chute was properly opened on 5,000 . . . beginning emergency procedures in

157

case of a malfunction on 6,000. . . . If everything was in order, I should then look around below for the airport and use my toggles to guide my descent.

When we were practicing this procedure on the ground earlier, there were several jokes told that I'm sure are standard among rookie jumpers. Like the one about the stutterer . . . jumping for the first time without a static line . . . rocketing earthward . . . counting: wu . . . wu . . . wu . . . one . . . th . . . th . . . th . . . th . . . th . . . thousand . . . t . . . t . . . t . . . t . . . two . . . th . . . th . . . th . . . th . . .

"JUMP!"

I'm not certain, but I think the jump master had to yell "jump" twice. I was so dazed with fear and awe that it was impossible for me to be certain about anything. Everything was a blur . . . distant. I was in a situation that called for a clear mind and precise physical coordination. But the wind was blinding me, my pulse was roaring in my ears, and my brain was short-circuiting. I wasn't even sure whether the command to jump had come from the jump master or from my imagination. I had lost almost all perspective on where I was and what I was doing.

Thus immobilized, I abandoned myself to the inevitable and let go of the plane.

And at that moment . . . the most intense point of the most unusual experience of my life . . . I passed out.

I have no memory of free-falling, or of the static line opening my parachute. The next thing I knew, I was sitting in the sky, all alone, bathed in the sun's last light. Instantly, I experienced the greatest rush of relief that I have ever felt in my life. It was at least equal in intensity to the terror I had felt only seconds before. What an adrenaline explosion!

As the rush subsided and my brain and senses began returning to normal, the first thing I noticed was the quiet. Except for an almost imperceptible whisper of wind through my helmet, I was in a world that was thick with silence. No birds chirping, no crickets, no traffic sounds . . . nothing. You'd have to be high, either in a parachute or a glider or up on a mountain, to know what it's like. Not even a soundproof room can recreate that genuine quiet, caused by being so far above the source of sound that it has died before it can reach you.

Then I looked down for the first time, and what I saw completely disoriented me. I had never been so far off the ground before, with nothing between me and the ground but air. It's not at all like looking down from a tall building or an airplane. I felt utterly insecure, knowing that the only thing holding me there was a contraption of cloth and buckles, and I tightened my grip on the straps.

But the insecurity gradually subsided as I began to enjoy my unusual new perspective. As I looked down, my legs and feet were huge compared to the details of the world below. I felt like Gulliver looking down on Lilliput. For as far as I cared to look, I could see little winding lines of roads, tiny farm buildings, diminutive hills and forests, all softened by a dark green haze. There was even a train on a distant hill, which made it all look for a moment like a perfectly detailed model train scene. And this whole miniature green world, laid out on a slightly convex surface, no longer seemed like my world. Even the

SOMETIMES YOU JUST HAVE TO STAND NAKED

sunset, off to my left, looked like it belonged to the world down there and not to the one I was in. I had never looked down at a sunset before. On the edge of all that green, the small mound of sun that remained was pulsing red.

So far, I had no sensation of downward motion. It was as if I could sit up there, ignored by gravity, for as long as I wanted. The world below me was so remote that it didn't seem I'd ever return to it. And I didn't care. I loved where I was, suspended thousands of feet above reality in a silent new world. And for those few moments, everything . . . the earth, the sun, myself . . . seemed frozen in time, as still as a snapshot.

Then, out of the corner of my eye, I saw my green plastic dummy rip cord in its place in the harness on the right side of my chest. The reason for pulling a dummy rip cord during the brief free-fall is to demonstrate that you have the presence of mind to eventually jump without a static line. Thinking my jump master might not have noticed that I hadn't pulled it when I was supposed to, I eased it out of the harness and stuck it in the pocket of my overalls.

Then I remembered that I was supposed to look for the airport. I couldn't find it at first, and a tinge of anxiety intruded on my high. Then I spotted it behind (and, of course, below) me. The awkwardness of trying to keep my eye on it by bending over and looking between my legs reminded me to use the toggles, in the straps an arm's reach above my shoulders, to control my direction.

I reached up and found both of the wooden toggle handles and pulled on the right one to see what would happen. Suddenly I was making a sweeping turn to the right. Then I pulled long and hard on the left toggle and began a full sweeping turn to the left.

I continued playing like this, stopping occasionally to lose myself in the sunset and scenery, until I noticed that the earth had moved closer. Then I began looking for something I should have located earlier, the white arrow.

The white arrow is what the people on the ground use to guide the jumper to the target. The target is a circle of pea gravel about twenty feet across and shaped like a pitcher's mound. The person at the arrow judges the wind and the jumper's position, and aims the arrow in the direction he thinks the jumper should face in order to move with or against the wind and land as near the target as possible. Each time he turns the arrow, the jumper is supposed to pull on one of his toggles until he is facing the same direction.

By now the fun of the jump was over. The earth was approaching more and more rapidly, and I had to think not only about which direction to face but also how to land.

I have already explained about the importance of keeping feet together and knees slightly bent and executing the five-point roll immediately on impact. In addition, we had been told we should not look at the ground as we approached it. I remembered our instructor saying, "It's impossible to judge exactly when you're going to hit. And if you hit before or after you're expecting to, you're likely to be so off guard you'll break a leg." Rather than look at the ground, he told us to "look out at the horizon and be ready to execute the five-point roll as soon as you feel impact."

I saw that I was going to miss the target by thirty to fifty yards. Not bad for a first jump. But below me was a barbed wire fence, which made me want to watch where I was going rather than look at the horizon. Then, about twenty yards from impact, I saw that I was going to miss the fence. So I quickly lifted my eyes to the horizon and tried to remember what to do when I landed to keep from breaking my leg again.

Suddenly I felt a jolt in my legs, lost my balance and fell backwards onto my butt. I had forgotten completely about the five-point roll.

I sat there for a moment in the fading light, delighted to be back on earth, safe and unbroken. At the same time I was trying to retain the high that I'd been feeling. But these were quickly replaced by an irresistible surge of pride. I'd done it!

With a broad grin cracking my face, I rolled over onto my knees and began slowly pulling in the lines of my chute.

❀ ❀ ❀

Well, that's it . . . almost; I'm planning to write an epilogue in the last chapter. But, y'know what? Here I am, almost finished with this story—and this book—and what I find myself thinking about more and more is all the things I could have done to make it better. I've even started jotting down ideas for next year's rewrite. I think this is happening because while I'm writing this book I learn more about the craft of writing than I'm able to incorporate into my own. And I learn things when I'm working on these later chapters that I wish I'd known when I was writing the earlier ones. It's the same for you, I'm sure. But I guess if we'd known everything before, there wouldn't be much point in my writing this book or your reading it. Maybe if it wasn't a learning experience for both of us, it wouldn't be any good.

LOVEMAKING

Sometimes it's not so much a specific fact about writing that I learn but a new perspective that I run across or develop. There's one that I've been thinking about all evening. It's not an original idea, just one that's making more sense all the time. This is it: Interesting writing is like lovemaking . . . it's a pleasure (to read) from the beginning, it becomes increasingly pleasurable as it progresses, it produces a climax of pleasure, and it leaves you (the reader) satisfied. To see that in a slightly different perspective, substitute "interesting" for "pleasure": It's interesting from the beginning, it becomes increasingly interesting as it progresses, it produces a climax of interest, and it leaves you satisfied.

When I apply this concept to the skydiving story, I can see some of its weaknesses more clearly. I think the story has a moderately interesting beginning (back in Intro I); I opened with some of the concrete details of the beginning of the experience, the phone call and my reaction to it. But I could have done it better. Or I could have begun it differently, say with me out on the wing, then flash back to the beginning. If I did that well, the reader's interest should be piqued enough that he'd want to go back to the beginning with me and find out who this person is and what he's doing out on the wing of a plane with someone yelling "jump" at him.

The story moves along all right, and it does achieve a climax in the episode in this chapter. But there is a lot I could do to make it more interesting. I could tell less and show more by using more dialogue and thoughts, and more description of what I was seeing and hearing.

The end, and in a sense the episode in this chapter is the end, isn't right yet. It runs several pages after the main climax to another minor climax. I kind of like the ending image though . . . me on my knees grinning. But someone who knows infinitely more about writing than I do once said, "Beware of anything in your writing that you think is good; your judgment may be playing tricks on you." So I'll reserve judgment.

LITTLE THINGS MEAN A LOT

The readers would also experience more pleasure, and the story would be more interesting for them, if I would give more time and attention to images, analogies and the connotations, surprise-value and sounds of words. That would give readers little things to enjoy at the same time that they're enjoying the story as a whole. One place in the story where I did take such care with little things was in the episode in Chapter 5 when I was talking about falling into power lines. I said I had a vision of myself ". . . fried black and dangling beside a lonely highway." I chose those words for the sounds and for the picture they created. I thought you might enjoy imagining driving down a lonely highway and seeing that figure dangling there. I also thought it might give you a clear idea of the level of my anxiety.

In that same episode, when I was explaining what happened when I practiced opening my reserve parachute, I said ". . . the parachute spilled out like soft silk intestines onto the ground." That seemed to me to accurately describe the way it looked, while again suggesting something about my emotional condition.

I should have done a lot more of that . . . not so much that it would be obtrusive, but enough to give you interesting little pictures and verbal surprises on a fairly regular basis.

CARING

Another idea, which ties in with the idea that interesting writing is like lovemaking, has to do with the importance of caring. Just as lovers care about what they're doing and with whom they're doing it, so writers must care about what they're writing and for whom they're writing it. The more I care about . . . and the more care I take with . . . my subject and audience, the more likely it is that what I write will be interesting. If I care enough about my readers, I'll not only be thorough and precise . . . I'll also do whatever else I can to make it a pleasure for them to read.

WRITING EXERCISE _____

Imagine a scene and recreate it in writing . . . for the sole purpose of entertaining your favorite readers. Make them laugh, amaze them, terrify them, blow their minds, fulfill their fantasies . . . give them a healthy dose of *whatever* it is they would most like to have. Recreate the scene in such detail, with such vivid words, that your readers will be drawn into it and affected by it. Remember, this one's for the readers.

IT'S BEEN FUN

What I'm saying about the skydiving story and about writing in general also applies to this book. I need to look for ways to make it more of a pleasure to read. I've been working at making it interesting all along. But not until now have I had this clear perspective on what "interesting writing" means.

On the other hand, if every time I rewrite this book I learn more about how to improve it next time, I'll never finish it. There has to come a time when I can say, without feeling guilty, "There. You're not perfect but I refuse to spend the rest of my life working on you. There are too many other things I want to do. Good-bye. It's been fun. You're on your own now."

      ❦ ❦ ❦

SOMETIMES-YOU-JUST-HAVE-TO-STAND-NAKED PAUSE-FOR-THE-CAUSE. Excuse me a moment. I'm going to the nearest restroom and write this graffiti on the wall:

  Writers Make Better Lovers

TRUTH

I've also been thinking about truth lately, in relation to writing.

Specific truth (factual accuracy) is essential in most types of writing, like journalism, research, biography. The readers must be able to rely on the accuracy of every piece of information. They are depending on the writer to give them the true details. But in other kinds of writing, like fiction and the personal-experience writing you're creating, specific truth is less important than *general* truth.

Anyone who writes about his or her own experience could aim for specific truth and attempt to recreate exactly what happened, down to the most minute details. But no one with any sense would want to write something that long and detailed. And no reader would want to read it. It would be impossible to be that accurate anyway because we forget most of the details involved in any experience, and memory distorts many of the rest. So the writer first strays from specific truth by accidentally and intentionally leaving out most of the details of the original experience.

But that's all right because what the writer's trying to communicate is not specific truth but general truth. Simply, general truth is whatever it is about the person or experience that makes him or her or it interesting and meaningful and therefore worth writing about. It's the writer's general perspective on the subject, the point he or she wants to make. And it serves as a unifying force for the writing, determining what will be left out and what will be included. It also helps the writer determine what, if anything, to change, such as creating a different setting, changing characters' personalities and changing what was actually said.

If this selective attitude toward the truth bothers you, look at it this way: What difference does it make to your readers whether your details are true to the original experience? What do they care whether it all happened exactly as you say? All they expect is that it be believable . . . that the details of your characters and situations be true to life. Do you care whether the specific details in Greg's story, "Ice Cream Man," are true? Of course not. It's the general truth he's illustrating that matters. (If the purpose of writing is to clarify reality, and the purpose of creative writing is to illustrate general truths about reality, the creative writer must have the freedom and the good sense to strip away all that's irrelevant or unnecessary, add other realistic details, and shade them all to suit his or her purpose.)

I've taken many liberties with the specific truth of the skydiving story; I've left out most of the details, changed what was said and thought, created some details to replace ones I couldn't recall. And I've done it to make the general truth clearer. That truth, or theme, as I mentioned earlier, is that taking risks can cause people to understand themselves better and to grow.

MORE TRUTH

I could simply *tell* you the general truth I deduced from my skydiving experience: "Hey, did you know that taking risks can cause people to understand themselves better and to grow?" But that, like all generalizations, would only appeal to your mind. And to understand it, you'd have to supply your own example (story). So, instead, I write the story, which shows you both what I experienced and how it affected me, and which, if I do it well, entertains you. The story appeals not only to your mind but also to your senses and your emotions . . . to all of you.

Stories (examples) are always more interesting than generalizations. That's the truth.

❀ ❀ ❀

Tip #28

When you're writing, don't try to make your readers think about what a good writer you are. They should be thinking about the thing you're writing about . . . not about you. See yourself as a medium through which whatever it is you have to communicate passes. Make it clear; make it interesting. That's all.

Substance is what matters. If you have nothing interesting or meaningful to communicate . . . no story to tell, no knowledge or perspective to share, no opinion to argue . . . you have no reason to write. And anything you do write will be insignificant.

Style is a servant of substance, not a substitute for it.

❀ ❀ ❀

Tip #29

Your life is overflowing with substance. You have knowledge, opinions, experiences, perspectives which, if you could see their value, you would see as worthy of being shared in writing. No matter how "normal" your life has been, from it you have learned numerous lessons and undergone numerous changes. If they mean something to you, they have value. If you feel strongly about them, you should share them.

Why? Sometimes because you need to . . . such as when you need to unburden yourself, or when you need to be entertaining, or when you need to simply share something meaningful.

You also need to pass on substance for the benefit of your readers . . . to enlighten them, inform them, offer them new perspectives, entertain them.

It could even be argued that it's your responsibility as a human being to share what you've learned from life. And writing is the most effective way to reach large numbers of other human beings.

❀ ❀ ❀

Tip #30

When I read Kurt Vonnegut's novel, SLAPSTICK, I was impressed with something he said about his sister, who had recently died: "I had never told her so, but she was the person I had always written for. She was the secret of whatever artistic unity I had ever achieved. She was the secret of my technique. Any creation which has any wholeness and harmoniousness, I suspect, was made by an artist or inventor with an audience of one in mind."

Think about that. The better you know your audience, the more you know how to interest him or her. In a sense, your audience is as responsible for what you create as you are. Your audience helps establish the tone, helps determine what needs to be said and helps give it form.

& & & ⅋ ⅋ ⅋

VOCABULARY EXERCISE #11

List twenty verbs that describe ways to walk or run. Then, at the rate of a word a day, define the seven that you like best and that you're most likely to use, and use them in imaginative sentences. And, of course, use the word-definition-sentence format.

⅋ ⅋ ⅋

SUGGESTED PUBLIC WRITING #6

If you don't already have a subject you care to write about, consider this: Think about a person you know who is younger than you and who is having a problem you also once had but which you have learned to deal with. It might be a problem that person isn't even aware of. It might be a problem that he or she causes other people, a problem that he or she causes himself or herself or a problem that other people are causing him or her. If you don't know such a person, use your imagination and create one. Then, write a story which, if that person should happen to read it, might help him or her learn to deal with the problem.

You might choose a person who has no respect for older people or one whose shyness is causing him or her unhappiness. Or you might choose a person who can't laugh at himself or herself, who doesn't realize what a good person he or she is, or who doesn't appreciate what a good life he or she has. Whatever the problem is, be sure it's one you've experienced yourself, so you'll understand and care about both your subject and your audience.

You might base the story more or less on your own experience and in it show someone learning to deal with the problem. Or you might write a story in which you make *not* having the problem so attractive that the reader will find his or her own way to overcome it. The main character in the story could be yourself, someone like yourself or someone the opposite of youself. The experience(s) that you relate could be your own, one like your own, or one the opposite of your own. And you could tell the story in third person, or in first person as yourself or in first person as the character. (See the Writing Exercise on page 150.) Make these decisions on the basis of what will be most effective and interesting for the audience you have in mind.

A word of caution: Let the story speak for itself. Don't preach, moralize or generalize. Just tell the story.

ED'S ALTERNATE

I like that suggestion. But there are other ways to accomplish the same end. "Me's" suggestion basically calls for process analysis, with a strong dose of example. Using those same methods, I don't see why you couldn't effectively *explain* how a person with a problem like you used to have can overcome it. Just explain what you used to be like, what caused you to change and how you feel about the change.

If you don't like either approach to that suggestion, you could go back to the hat and draw out a new combination of rhetorical methods. (Remember our little game?) Maybe you'll be lucky and draw definition and examples, so you can write about your favorite activity. Or, classification, definition and examples, so you can write about *all* the things you like . . . or don't like.

Okay, you want something specific? How about using whatever methods you need to persuade some audience to accept your view of something. For example, you could argue the importance of personal self-sufficiency, the value of taking pride in your work, or who's going to win the NCAA Division I championship.

Lovers Make Better Writers

CHAPTER 13

techniques of fiction (the art of lying)

Eyes
Paula Itschner

"I don't want him to come home ever!" I cried as I tossed myself down on my canopy bed and snatched up my worn Pooh Bear. I wasn't sorry for what I said; I meant every word of it. I just couldn't understand how she would allow that man back in our house. It had been over two years since he had left. Could Mom have forgotten how much that man, my father, had put us through?

I recall his last night with us. It was like every other night, except that the yelling was a little louder. In self-defense, we had "I Love Lucy" on the tv as loud as it would go. Eileen, who was a year younger than me, was sitting directly in front of the television trying to hear only it. It was her favorite show, yet when Lucy fell in the green dye Eileen didn't even smile.

Jennifer and Susan shared a floral pillow at the side of the television. From the soft heaving of their backs, I could tell that they were asleep. I always wondered how they managed to sleep through the battles; it must have been an advantage of their age.

Suddenly the fighting stopped. Then the door crashed shut. Eileen had turned down the television and a silence was ringing through my ears. I sat staring at my older brother, Billy, who was next to me on the couch. He was only twelve but to me he was a tower of wisdom.

A cry pierced the silence—cutting into my head. It was Mom crying but not as she did so often after their fights; these were long wails of pain.

All I could think, as I vaulted over the back of the couch and dashed through the kitchen, was that he had hurt her. I stopped at the living room door; my heart was threatening to burst through my breastbone. Mom's back was bent over. Her slender hands partially covered her face; no bruises marked it. just an empty look of pain.

169

I fell into my mother's arms and for a moment, though I was only ten, I felt as if she was the child and I was consoling her. Feeling her back heave with sobs drew hate from deep within me. Hate for him, for anyone who would hurt her.

She reluctantly released me from her arms and stood unsurely. She managed a reassuring smile as I stared at her in silence. She appeared as always, her tall slender figure not showing a sign of the five children she had carried. Her soft blue eyes were accented by the short dark curls that framed her face.

The terror of the moment had vanished, or rather Mom had managed to hide it, as I followed her into the kitchen. No mention was made of the fight; hardly a word was spoken. She performed her motherly duties mechanically. The dishes were done, and Susan and Jennifer were tucked into bed along with Eileen who had also fallen asleep.

Billy and I were back on the plaid couch in the tv room when Mom came in and sat down between us. The tension in the room had become almost unbearable when Billy finally asked where Dad had gone. At first I thought Mom had not heard him. She coughed a little, and color seemed to drain from her face with every breath she expelled. This was so unlike the mother who had breezily answered every question from "Why is God invisible?" to "Where do babies come from?"

The answer began to come out in fragments. "Billy . . . Paula," she began, "sometimes married people have trouble getting along. Like your father and me." After a long explanation, the truth came out: "Your father isn't going to live here anymore." I know she said more but all I could hear were those words as they bounced in my head trying to find a place to escape.

Billy stood in front of Mom and flung accusations at her. "You don't care; you made him leave!" he cried. His voice broke and tears snuck from his eyes and ran down his cheeks. He started to fall into Mom's arms where he knew no pain was as bad. But he stopped, realizing he was being weak. Then he tore his stare from Mom and escaped to his room. As I watched him leave, I felt a tightness in my throat, and tears teased my eyes. I clung to the place Billy had left vacant and fought the salty tears until I fell asleep.

That night was quickly forgotten and the routine of life went on. Dad had gone to live with Grandma; we went to see him on weekends. At home things were normal with the usual scraped knees and tearful fights over going to bed. The only things lacking were the arguments that had seemed to start at precisely four o'clock when Dad came home from work. Mom didn't cry as much; lately her voice had even danced through the house at dinner time.

One night, months after Dad had left, the aroma of chicken carried me into the kitchen. I took my place on top of the noisy refrigerator where I had the best view of Mom cooking. This was my favorite time of the day because it was all mine. I would share my most precious secrets with Mom while she let me salt the food. I even told her about kissing Tommy Brown one night.

Tonight was different. Mom stared blankly down at the chicken. I didn't think she was going to talk; I didn't think she even knew I was there. She spoke without even looking up: "Paula, sweetheart." Her tone was soft and

SOMETIMES YOU JUST HAVE TO STAND NAKED

strained. "Paula, Billy and I just had a talk and he wants to go live with your father." Live with Dad? I couldn't understand; didn't he see that with Dad gone the pain was gone? How could Billy leave? My throat knotted and I was about to release the tightness in a flow of tears. A sharp pain stopped me; when I looked down I saw I had bitten through the skin on my hand.

I lashed out in the only way I knew. "I hate Dad! I wish he were dead!" I screamed. Mom's hand struck my face sharply before I had finished. Mom had never slapped me before and for a moment she stared at her hand as if it was forever marked. Then she warned me never to say that again and went on to tell me what a good father he was and how he loved me. I couldn't understand how he could love me yet hurt me so badly. I didn't hear anything except the humming refrigerator, the crackling chicken and my pounding heart.

Billy left on a bright summer day which I spent locked in my room to avoid Dad. I vowed from that day on never to see Dad again.

On Friday afternoons my three little sisters would dash out of the house to spend a couple of days with Dad. Late on Sunday they would bounce back home excited about the great times they'd had. But I didn't care. I spent the weekends with Mom experimenting in the kitchen, shopping or visiting relatives.

After one weekend with Dad, Eileen came home with a huge secret. She said she wasn't supposed to tell, but after sufficient bribery she told me. Grandma had said I was not allowed near her house because I was a terrible, selfish child. Eileen was ready for me to cry. I didn't, not even after my birthday came and Grandma didn't give me a present. After all, Dad was her son.

My life at school was affected too. Theresa Brown had been my best friend since the first grade. One day she came to school and wouldn't talk to me. When I asked her what was wrong, she said her mom had told her I was a bad influence and she would be grounded if she even talked to me. I decided it was time to get a new best friend.

The principal was worst of all. We called her Worm because she was so skinny. She came tapping on our religion class door every Tuesday and Thursday looking for me. I sat in the back of the classroom and had to walk past staring eyes and giggles to reach the door.

Sister never said a word as she led me out of the school and through the clunking metal doors into the dark church. There we would kneel on the icy marble floor with bleeding Jesus before us and Mary and Joseph's dead eyes watching us. Sister closed her eyes and counted the beads with her wrinkled hands as her prayers echoed off the walls.

Once I asked her what we were praying for. She shook her head from side to side and looked down at me with pity-filled eyes. She explained it was for my "sinful" parents. I didn't need to ask what they had done; I knew what she thought. I clenched my hands and counted the lines on the floor until the rosary ended. I never told Mom about prayer days because I didn't want her to think she was a sinner.

During the two years following the separation, Mom dated two men. One of them had grey hair and they played Scrabble. The other man had blond hair and she would go riding in his red convertible. It was only fair; Dad had moved into a new house with Billy, a cat, two dogs and his blonde girlfriend.

Then things began to change. Mom and Dad began dating each other and going away together.

"Paula, your father is going to be here in a minute." Well, I hadn't seen him in nearly a year and I didn't want to see him now. I went to the window and had one leg out when I spied Pooh Bear. I grabbed him by the leg but decided a near-teenager should go it alone so I flung him back. I jumped out of the window onto the hot driveway and ran barefoot until my house was out of sight.

I wasn't planning to run away for good, just until Dad left. I searched around and found a comfortable spot in front of an old maple tree a safe two blocks away.

Lost in a daydream, I didn't notice the car drive up. I looked up to a tall man with receding black hair and broad shoulders. His face was cleanly shaven, his lips unmoving, his nose long and stern. His eyes were wide and brown. They were my eyes, my eyes. I didn't want to see my eyes on this man, so I ran. I pounded over yard after yard until I felt a strong hand grab my arm.

I screamed with pain, not from the grip of the hand but from the scars of the past. He was the cause of it all; he had caused everything to fall apart.

My hands beat against his chest as I screamed, "I hate you, I hate you!"

Everything stopped suddenly. My body was quivering to control itself but my eyes were fixed on him. Tears were coming from his eyes, my eyes, but they seemed so old and weak.

At that moment I saw that he too had suffered the same pain I had. He wasn't to blame; no one was. The hate I had felt was washed away as I cried for the first time in two years. I held my daddy and I cried.

※   ※   ※

Each time I read Paula's story I notice something else that causes me to admire it even more. Like the way she described her mother's crying: long wails of pain. The long-A sounds echo off each other until I can almost *hear* her painful wailing. I also like the way she weaves the other kids into the story by describing where they were and what they were doing. That's much more effective than saying, "There were five of us kids, four girls and a boy. Our ages were. . . ."

But generally what makes her story so effective is the storytelling methods she used. They are the same methods writers of fiction use. These methods, or techniques, include plot, characterization, setting, symbols, style, point of view and theme.

PLOT

A basic ingredient of effective fiction or any other successful writing is structure (form) . . . the way it moves readers from the beginning to the end, without losing them along the way. In fiction, the most common structure is plot.

SOMETIMES YOU JUST HAVE TO STAND NAKED

Plot, generally, traces someone's conflict from its beginning through its resolution. Paula's conflict is brought on by the disruption of her family. Her parents' separation and her attachment to her mother cause her to try to shut out her father and all feelings for him. This causes more problems, and her conflict finally reaches a climax when her father confronts her under the maple tree. At that point, she admits him back into her life rather than try to maintain her self-defeating hatred. And as she resolves her conflict she begins to see things in a more realistic perspective.

The main conflict in a story can be either inside the main character or between that character and someone or something else. In the skydiving story, the main conflict is mostly internal, between my *desire* to jump and my *fear* of the consequences. But there is also external conflict, between my well-being and all those things that threaten it: malfunctions, the hard ground, gravity. The conflicts build in intensity until I'm outside the plane hanging onto the strut. This is the story's climax, the point at which I must resolve the conflict, either by climbing back into the plane or throwing my fate to the wind.

Stories are based on conflict because conflict is such a common and meaningful ingredient of all people's lives. Our lives are filled with conflict from the moment we awaken until we next retreat to sleep. How many times today, for example, have you faced, and resolved, a should-I-or-shouldn't-I conflict? We resolve most of our conflicts routinely and with little effort. But some give us great difficulty, and as a result of dealing with them we are somehow changed; we've learned something that affects the way we think or act. This natural process is what almost all stories are based on: people dealing with problems, and learning and changing as a result.

When you are planning a writing, whether it's based on an experience, a person or a fantasy, look for the possibility of structuring it around a conflict or problem that develops to a climax and is resolved. If you can't build it on a conflict, then try something like a series of examples or incidents that are increasingly interesting. In a conflict story, the readers want to find out what happens or how the character handles what happens. In a nonconflict writing, the readers read on because they're finding that the further they read the more interesting it becomes.

Now, pull out a writing you're currently working on, preferably one that could be written as a story. Would plotting make it more effective? More interesting? Could it be built on the development and resolution of a conflict? If not, is there some way you could arrange (structure) it so that it becomes increasingly interesting?

CHARACTERIZATION

Think of characterization as the act of presenting the readers with interesting people for whom they come to have some feeling . . . as they watch those people attempt to deal with their problems. In most stories, the focus is mainly on one person. The writer shows what that person's like, and shows him or her encountering a meaningful problem, attempting to cope with the problem and finally being affected by it all.

There are two ways to present the people in your stories, directly and indirectly. You present a character directly when you *tell* the readers what kind of person he or she is. (He was afraid of dogs.) You present a character indirectly (dramatically) when you let what he or she says and thinks and does *show* what kind of person he or she is. ("Get that dog away from me!" he cried, cowering behind his host.) The most effective method, of course, is to show rather than tell. Then the readers can see for themselves rather than having to rely on what they're told. It's more interesting for them to read, too, because they feel they're learning about a real person rather than someone else's idea of that person. Most stories use both methods but rely primarily on the indirect because it's more effective and it's what readers enjoy most.

You learn about Paula indirectly; you form your own idea about what kind of person she is by observing what she thinks, says and does. Notice how much she has shown of herself. And ask yourself how much less effective her story would be if she weren't willing to stand so naked. Her story is interesting precisely because she's open about intimate and painful experiences and feelings, including hate for her father. And she doesn't just tell you she hated him; she shows herself saying it: "I hate you, I hate you!"

Now, look at the main character in that writing of yours and assess how much the readers know about him or her (or you). Do the readers know enough to understand what you want them to understand? Can they see the character? Hear the character? Understand his or her feelings?

SETTING

Setting is where the story takes place, the stage on which it unfolds. The more clearly the readers can see where it's taking place, the more they enjoy and become involved in it. Some stories have more detailed settings than others, depending on how important setting is to the story. As a general rule, describe enough of the setting to give the readers at least a sketchy picture.

You can use the setting to reflect something about the main character's nature or situation, too. For example, if the character is fearful you could color the details of setting so that they appear subtly frightening: gnarled limbs, darkness, cold winds, that sort of thing.

You can also use setting to establish mood. For example, if you're writing about something pleasant you could describe the setting as sunny and green.

SOMETIMES YOU JUST HAVE TO STAND NAKED

Check that writing of yours for setting. Would more details of setting make it more effective? Could it be described in a way that hints at the nature of the character and helps set the mood of the story?

I could use setting more effectively in the skydiving story. For example, I could give a brief description of the room I was sitting in when the phone rang, and do it in such a way that it would show not only where I was but also hint at what kind of person I am and what was going to happen. But to do it effectively, I'd probably have to change the point of view to third person.

POINT OF VIEW

Point of view is another term for the narrator, the voice telling the story. The voice may be that of the writer, that of a personality created by the writer to tell the story or that of a major or minor character in the story. And the voice can be speaking either in first or third person.

A first person narrator is usually the main character in the story, like Paula in her story and me in the skydiving story, telling about what happened to him or her or what he or she did. A first person narrator can also be a minor character telling about his or her experience with someone else. This is the point of view Greg used in "Ice Cream Man." And it's the point of view you may have used in your own writings about other people.

A third person narrator is someone not in the story who shows and tells what happened. (See the hunting story, "Life in the Woods," which I began back in Intro II . . . and which, if all goes well, I'll finish in Chapter 14.) Third person point of view makes possible, for the writer, a distance and objectivity that are difficult if not impossible with first person, especially when the character in the story is more or less the writer. And third person makes it possible for the writer to say things that would be awkward or embarrassing to say with first person. It's awkward to describe yourself in a story using first person. (I'm five-seven with curly brown hair, a beautiful face and an outstanding figure.) It's easy using third person. (She was five-seven with curly brown hair, a beautiful face and an outstanding figure.) It can be embarrassing to talk about yourself in first person; it's easy in third person, when you seem to be talking about someone else. And once you've begun, you'll probably feel freer to change yourself (the character) if you think it will make the story more effective.

In that writing of yours that I keep referring to, if you're using a first person narrator (telling the story yourself), experiment with third person and notice the difference it makes in what you can say and show.

If I were to tell the skydiving story from a third person point of view . . . and describe the setting more effectively, as I was saying earlier . . . it would go something like this:

The only person in the dimly-lit, cluttered room sat in an old stuffed chair in the corner. Long dark hair and a beard nearly obscured his face, which was tilted toward the paperback novel in his lap. Bob Dylan was halfway through "It's All Right, Ma . . . I'm Only Bleeding" when the phone rang in the next room.

No point of view is inherently more effective than another. Each has its advantages and limitations. The decision about which to use should be based on the nature of the story you have to tell and the effect you want to have on your readers.

SYMBOLS

Symbols are subtle ways of adding complexity and suggestiveness to what you're writing. Like details, examples and especially analogies, they're a way of saying a lot with a few words. They are hints rather than explanations.

Usually symbols reinforce something about the character or situation. In Paula's story, for example, flinging Pooh Bear back into the room symbolizes the childish behavior she's about to fling off when she reunites with her father. In the skydiving story, the sun shining on me ("bathed in the sun's last light") symbolizes the way I'm feeling at that moment. It also foreshadows a happy ending. If it wasn't going to be a happy ending, I might have given you clouds or near-darkness to prepare you for it. Thus, symbolic details are what they are literally (a Pooh Bear, a sunset) and they also reflect or hint at something else.

Names can be symbolic. For example, Frieda for free . . . April for innocent . . . Charley Owlsly for wise . . . Buck for macho. . . . Colors can also be symbolic. Black is often a symbol for death, white for purity, red for passion or danger. Seasons and times of the day can be symbols. Spring and morning are frequently used to symbolize youth, beginnings. Fall and evening can symbolize old age, endings. Anything can be a symbol. And usually if you see it as one, you'll give it enough subtle emphasis to make it work, even though your readers aren't consciously aware of its contribution to the effect of the story.

Now check your story for symbols. If it doesn't have any, work in one or two just for the practice.

STYLE (IRONY)

You've already heard plenty about style in this book, and you've been working on your own all along. There's one more element of style I'd like to call your attention to, though: irony.

Irony occurs when the writer says something other than what he or she literally means (verbal irony) . . . or gives you something you weren't expecting (cosmic or situation irony) . . . or makes you aware of something which the character is not aware of (dramatic irony).

I'm being verbally ironic when I say, on a gloomy rainy day, "Fine weather we're having!" What I mean, literally, is "This weather sucks!"

There is situation irony in Paula's story when her hate gives way to tears, something she hadn't expected.

Dramatic irony occurs when the readers have a more accurate perception of the person who's telling the story than that person has of himself or herself. For example, he (the first person narrator) might think he's coming across as cool and together while the readers (and the author) see him as a dolt who doesn't have a clear concept of himself. You also have dramatic irony when you see what's going to happen but the character to whom it's going to happen doesn't. For example, you see a bunch of bad guys waiting behind a clump of trees and your hero, Roy Rogers, riding unsuspectingly toward their ambush. "Look out, Roy!"

Now check that story of yours for irony, especially situation irony. Why? Because irony of situation . . . the unexpected . . . is one of the things that makes life (and therefore writing) interesting. You're expecting a C in writing but your instructor gives you a B; that's ironic. Someone you're sure doesn't even know you exist asks you for a date; how ironic. You're taking your girlfriend home to break up with her but you break your leg instead and end up marrying her. Isn't life ironic!

By playing the expected against the unexpected, irony puts an edge on what you're writing that increases the readers' enjoyment. Study it, and use it when you can.

THEME

Theme can simply be the purpose you're trying to accomplish in a writing. For example, my purpose in writing the skydiving story was to show you how frightening it was for me. More specifically, though, theme is the general truth which a story illustrates, the point that everything in the story works together to make. As I said earlier, the skydiving story illustrates the theme that taking risks can result in growth. The *purpose* of Paula's story is to show how her parents' separation disrupted her life. The story's *theme* is that rejection and even hatred can be broken down and replaced by love.

Does that story of yours have a theme beyond its purpose? Does it illustrate a general truth? The more your writing means, the more interesting it will be.

        ❀   ❀   ❀

My explanations of the techniques of fiction are not exhaustive; like most of the explanations in this book, they are intended to be introductory and suggestive. If you find something that appears useful you should explore it further.

❀ ❀ ❀

VOCABULARY COMMENCEMENT

Surely by now you've developed the word-a-day habit and are convinced of its value. From now on, keep your words to yourself. Except, of course, when you write.

❀ ❀ ❀

STYLE SELF-ANALYSIS COMMENCEMENT

This time, list *every* strength you can find in your style, including strengths you mentioned in previous analyses. Then list every weakness which you have nearly or completely eliminated. Finally, list every weakness which you still need to work on. Don't do this hastily. Think about it for several days, adding to each list whenever you think of another strength or weakness.

❀ ❀ ❀

SUGGESTED PUBLIC WRITING #7

This is it . . . your last chance . . . your last writing assignment, suggested or otherwise. (Is that a tear in your eye?)
  Write a story. Base it more or less on your own experience(s) or on a dream or favorite fantasy. And use as many of the techniques presented in this chapter as you can to make it the most effective and meaningful writing you've ever created. Make it a story you would enjoy reading. (If there's a story you've been carrying inside you for days—or years—make that the one you write for this suggestion. You may never have a better opportunity.)

❀ ❀ ❀

ED'S ALTERNATE

Think of yourself as a valid spokesperson on a particular subject as the result of your experience of it. Then, using persuasion, analysis and examples, express your view and convince others of its validity by recreating the circumstances that led you to adopt it.

It's the truth even if it didn't happen.

Ken Kesey
One Flew Over the Cuckoo's Nest

CHAPTER 14

through you,
not from you

Me: Well, Ed . . . I've really done it this time.

Ed: What's wrong? You're almost finished, aren't you?

Me: Yeah, and that's part of the problem. You remember that story I started way back in Intro II? The one about the eight-year-old boy named Mark. .. .

Ed: . . . going hunting with his grandpa? Yeah, I remember. I was beginning to think you'd forgotten about it, though.

Me: I wish I could. The main reason I put the start of it in the book in the first place was to force myself to write the rest of it. But I haven't been able to. I've worked on it all along, and I have plenty of notes and ideas, but I can't figure out how to tell it.

Ed: Why don't you just forget it? I'm sure no one would care.

Me: Naw, I can't do that.

Ed: I didn't think so. Well, if you're determined to do it, let's figure out what's hanging you up. Any ideas?

Me: I'm not sure. I just know that writing this story is not the same as writing the skydiving story. I don't feel free to be myself when I write it. And everything I write sounds stupid.

Ed: Maybe the problem is with the third person narrator you're using. Why don't you try telling it in your own voice, with you as the main character: first person point of view?

Me: I've tried that. It didn't work either. I guess the basic problem is that it's not a true story. It's made up of elements from several different places and times, mixed with some that exist only in my imagination. Mark is me, but he's also partly my kids, especially Jude. And Grandpa is my grandpa, but he's also partly my dad, mixed with a lot of myself.

Ed: If it didn't really happen, why are you telling it?

Me: Because it means something. And it did happen; it just didn't all happen to Grandpa and to a kid named Mark on his eighth birthday.

(Jude enters the room.)

Jude: Hi. What're you doing?

Me: Talking to Ed.

Jude: Ed? Where? Who's Ed?

Me: Somebody in my head.

Jude: Oh. What're you talking to him about?

Me: A story I'm trying to write.

Jude: Do you want to read one I just wrote?

Me: Sure.

(Jude hands Me a notebook. The story snakes down one page. It's written in red ink. Several words in the middle are swollen, probably by a drop of slobber that escaped in a moment of concentration.)

Jude's story: Once upon a time
there was a cocker
spaniel. He was kind of
a rich dog. He wore a
dark brown collar with
diamonds on it. He only
wore that one when he
was in the house. When
he went outside he wore
a collar that any dog
would ware. His

SOMETIMES YOU JUST HAVE TO STAND NAKED

name was Keeper. His
mothers name was Maggie.
One day Keeper was
out playing and he
saw something
it was something poisonous
it looked good
so he ate it. He died about
15 minutes later. When his
owners found out
they were sad.

Me: That's good, Jude.

Jude: It's part true and part made up. D'you like it, really?

Me: Yeah, I do. I wish it was longer, though. I'd like to know Keeper better, and the people he lived with.

Jude: I couldn't think of anything else. Maybe I'll work on it some more later. Have you seen my gun?

Me: It's over there by the fireplace.

Jude: Thanks.

Me: Thank *you.*

Ed: That was an interesting coincidence: you and Jude are both writing stories that are "part true and part made up."

Me: Yeah, but when I try to add "made up" details to mine they come out trite, melodramatic, boring.

Ed: Maybe that's because you're not really "making up" those details; maybe they're coming from memories you have of other stories you've read, or from tv or movies. You have to go beyond memory to creative imagination . . . if you want your writing to be original.

Me: I think you're on to something.

Ed: Good. And make yourself believe the story really happened. Tell it to yourself over and over until it feels right. And spend more time getting to know your characters. Maybe part of the reason you can't be yourself is because you don't know the story well enough yet.

Me: That makes sense.

Ed: Try this, too. Forget about it being *your* story. Instead, see it as a story that exists outside of you and which you are in a position to tell because it bears strong resemblance to incidents in your own life. It's like Dylan says about his songs: They come through him, not from him.

Me: Boy, you're full of good advice tonight, Ed. I didn't know you had it in you.

Ed: You haven't been listening.

℣ ℣ ℣

Dear Reader: Before reading what follows, flip back to Intro II and read it again. Think of it as a prologue to what's coming; it's not essential to the finished story but it will help orient you.

Life in the Woods *(continued)*

II

"Ready?" Grandpa asked as he pushed open the screen door.

"Yeah," said Mark. "I'll go get the guns and meet you at the gate."

As Mark trotted toward the car, Grandpa stepped off the porch . . . and felt his mind begin to slide. "Not now," he pleaded. "Not today." He knew it was senility. He'd been having spells for over a year. They only lasted a few moments, but they always left him frightened and disoriented.

He had enjoyed his life. But now he saw it all threatened. Who wanted to spend time with a frightened, forgetful old man? Gradually he had come to view age as his enemy, and Mark as his salvation. He was convinced that somehow through Mark he could be reborn.

Ironically, Mark, the only child of an overprotective mother, saw Grandpa as *his* salvation, not just from the restrictions imposed by his mother, but from most of the limitations of his age. In the past year he had managed to dodge several of his mother's obstacles with the aid and encouragement of his increasingly lenient grandpa. He had built birdhouses with Grandpa's power tools, chopped wood with an ax, fished off the dam, even drunk a little of Grandpa's homemade wine. His intent today was to fire the shotgun.

III

Grandpa latched the gate and picked up his shotgun, which Mark had left leaning against the fence. When he turned in the direction of the woods, he saw Mark, already well ahead of him, his features softened by the haze that hung like a low cloud over the pasture.

As Grandpa looked at Mark he saw himself. The brown hair, the thin, handsome face, the lean body were his at that age. He had even stood in this same pasture, very likely in the same spot Mark was standing now. And if he could, he would have traded places with him.

"Wait for me," he called.

Mark stopped and looked back. Then he raised his BB gun and began

SOMETIMES YOU JUST HAVE TO STAND NAKED

pelting the greenish brown cowpiles that littered the pasture. As his accuracy improved, he tried to shoot the tops off the little mushrooms that were growing out of the piles.

When Grandpa had almost caught up with him, Mark ran ahead again, firing from the hip until the gun was empty. Then he stopped to reload. When he finished, he looked back and chuckled. Grandpa was still twenty-five yards back, jolting along in his awkward, flat-footed gait. His features were partly obscured by a two-month growth of whiskers. Silky white hair hung and waved about his face. Mark liked Grandpa's beard; he liked his hair even more. The longer it was, the better. Already it was over his collar and covering his ears. Grandma was displeased with his shaggy look, but Grandpa decided he didn't care; from now on he was going to do what he wanted.

By the time he caught up with Mark, the sun had burned through the thin clouds. It was a clear, crisp fall morning.

As they walked side by side, Grandpa brushed his hand across Mark's curly brown hair, tossling it slightly. Sensing an opportunity, Mark looked up at him and said, "Want me to carry your gun for a while?"

Grandpa knew that Mark would be trying to get his hands on the shotgun.

"Maybe," he answered.

"When?" asked Mark.

"I said *maybe,*" Grandpa teased.

A crow landed about twenty yards to their left, on one of the jimson-weeds that stood resolutely throughout the pasture. Mark fired several shots at the crow and finally annoyed it enough that it flew about fifteen yards farther away. Then he turned and trotted off after Grandpa, who was now almost to the stream that separated the pasture from the woods.

IV

"I'll cross first," said Grandpa. "Then I'll give you a hand."

Grandpa stepped across the stream carefully, holding on to a low-hanging branch of the thorn tree that rose from the edge of the water. Then he turned to give Mark a hand . . . and froze, his hand extended and his mouth open, staring into the tiny hole of Mark's BB gun.

"Mark!"

Pfftt.

"Ahhhh!" cried Grandpa, his face distorted with the pain he antici-pated. But the thought of pain was quickly overshadowed by something even more disturbing: that was himself standing there pointing the gun.

"Above your head, Grandpa!"

"What?" he croaked, jerking around. Hanging directly above him was a bright gold and green snake. And in the middle of its forehead was Mark's BB.

"Jesus," moaned Grandpa, easing his quaking body to the bank of the stream.

"I got him!" shouted Mark. "Look. I shot him right between the eyes."

"Give me the gun," growled Grandpa.

"Huh?"

"I said, give me that gun."

Then Mark noticed that Grandpa was white and shaking.

"Grandpa, I-I'm sorry. I didn't mean to scare you. All I saw was the snake."

Grandpa was silent for a moment. His nerves were beginning to calm, but his temper wasn't; his white eyebrows were arched to points.

"What the hell's wrong with you, boy? Why'd you want to shoot a garter snake?"

"I-I didn't know what kind it was," said Mark.

"You know there's no poisonous snakes around here. Besides, you could have shot my eye out. And you want me to let you carry the shotgun? I'd have to be crazy."

Mark was afraid to say anything. He walked along the stream a little way, then turned and looked longingly into the woods. It was a large woods. But it wasn't thick, and he could see sunny clearings where late wild flowers still bloomed.

"Mark."

He turned and walked slowly back to where Grandpa was sitting.

"Mark, I'm not going to let this spoil your birthday. Just promise me you'll be more careful."

"I will," he said quickly. "I'm sorry, Grandpa."

"Oh, get rid of that long face. It was a hell of a shot. I'm just glad you were carrying your gun and not mine."

V

"All right, now, it's time to be quiet," Grandpa said as they entered the woods. "No more talking or target shooting. Walk a few yards ahead of me and keep your eyes and ears alert."

As they walked Indian-file toward the heart of the woods, Grandpa tried not to think about the disturbing vision of himself he'd seen back at the stream. Instead he tried to think about Mark. His mother should see him now, he thought.

"Dad, I wish you weren't so set on taking him hunting," she had said that morning. They were sitting in the kitchen waiting for Mark to come down. "It's bad enough your giving him a BB gun."

"There's nothing to worry about," he had assured her. "It's not the hunting that's important, anyway."

"Then why don't you leave the guns home and just take a walk in the woods?"

"Honey," he said, patting her shoulder, "stop smothering him. You're going to make him as scared of life as you are."

Mark stopped to look up into a large oak for signs of squirrels, and Grandpa stumbled against him with a grunt.

"Grandpa!"

"Uh . . . sorry," muttered Grandpa. "Did you want to stop for a while? Here, let's sit on this log."

SOMETIMES YOU JUST HAVE TO STAND NAKED

Scanning the woods carefully, hoping to see large squirrels appear at any moment, Mark said, "Grandpa, you used to live on this farm, didn't you?"

"Uh-huh, grew up here. Practically lived in these woods when I was your age. There were so many squirrels in here then you could almost hunt 'em with a stick."

"It's really neat out here. Why'd you move into town?"

"Oh, the farm wasn't big enough for Grover and me both to make a living off. And I didn't want to spend my life eating poor man's food."

"What's poor man's food?" Mark asked.

"Beans 'n shit," said Grandpa laughing.

Mark laughed too. He liked it when Grandpa cussed, which he'd been doing more and more lately, even around Grandma, who didn't like it at all.

"Well, c'mon," said Grandpa. "I know a good spot further in."

"Want me to carry your gun yet?" asked Mark as he picked up his own.

"No, thanks."

They hadn't walked twenty feet before Grandpa was deep in thought. Soon he was a boy again, walking in the woods with his father.

"I wish I was older," he heard himself say. His father didn't answer.

"I said, I wish I was older," Mark said. He had stopped and turned to face Grandpa. "I'd have my own shotgun, and I could shoot it any time I wanted."

"Don't wish your life away," Grandpa heard his father say. "Enjoy your youth; you'll grow up soon enough."

Mark had heard these words before, but the dreamlike tone of Grandpa's voice troubled him. Something wasn't right.

Suddenly, taking a step toward Mark, Grandpa felt something strike his leg. His shotgun fell to the ground as both of his hands shot out in front of him and grabbed ahold of Mark's hair.

"Aaaa . . .," squealed Mark, dropping his own gun and tearing at Grandpa's fingers. On his toes in agony, he turned just enough to unload a kick to Grandpa's shin. As suddenly as the assault had begun, it ended, as Grandpa released his grip on Mark's hair to minister to this real pain in his leg.

"Why'd you do that?" Mark demanded, brushing tears from his cheeks. Then he noticed Grandpa's wild eyes. "Grandpa . . . are you all right?"

Grandpa hobbled a few steps to a fallen tree, sat, and pulled up his right pants leg.

"Grandpa, what's wrong?"

Grandpa twisted his leg and inspected his calf, quickly at first, then slowly and thoughtfully. After about half a minute, he glanced up at Mark. He looked confused. "A snake bit me . . . but there's no mark. Right here," he said weakly, pointing to his calf.

"A snake?" Mark said.

Grandpa stood and walked slowly back to where the shotgun was lying in the grass. Before picking it up, he examined the ground carefully. His search stopped when he saw a curved branch lying across his path. As if he knew what would happen, he stepped on one end of the branch. When he did, the other end flipped up out of the grass.

"I guess it was just this stick," he said sheepishly. "I'm sorry, Mark. Did I hurt you?"

"Ye . . . nah, you just pulled my hair a little. Did I hurt you when I kicked you?"

"Worse'n the snake," said Grandpa, forcing a smile.

As they were picking up their guns, Mark said, "Grandpa, if there aren't any poisonous snakes out here, why'd you . . . ?"

"I don't know. I guess you got me so nervous back there at the stream, all I could think was snake when that stick hit me."

"It scared you, didn't it?" Mark said.

"Of course it scared me. Why else would I try to pull your hair out?" As he said this, he stroked Mark's hair, some of which was still twisted out of place.

"Here, you want to carry this a while?" Grandpa asked, offering Mark the shotgun. "You can carry it if you promise not to tell your mom about it, or about me stepping on that stick."

"Can I tell her about the snake I shot?"

"Uh . . . no, I wouldn't tell her that either."

"I'm not going to have much to tell her when she asks what we did, am I?" said Mark, handing Grandpa his BB gun and taking ahold of the shotgun with both hands. It was much heavier than his BB gun, but it was welcome weight.

VI

They walked in silence for a while, broken occasionally by Grandpa calling directions to Mark, who was still walking in the lead. After about fifteen minutes, they entered a sunlit clearing. A small tree trunk lay along one side.

"This looks like a good spot," called Grandpa softly. "Let's sit on that trunk and see if we can't hear some squirrels."

"If we spot one, can I shoot at it with your gun?"

"I don't know," said Grandpa. "We'll see."

Mark sat still and listened, cradling the shotgun. After a couple of minutes he whispered, "I can't hear anything."

"Listen to the trees," said Grandpa. "Listen for nuts and shells falling through the leaves. There ought to be lots of squirrels feeding up in these big old oaks."

After a few more minutes of hearing nothing but birds, Mark said, "I'm hungry. Can we eat something now?"

"Good idea," whispered Grandpa.

They ate some of the sandwiches and apples Grandpa had stored in the pouch of his hunting jacket, and drank water from Mark's canteen. They were silent while they ate. But Grandpa's brain wasn't.

"You still want to shoot that cannon?" he asked finally.

"Sure."

"Well, y'know, it kicks like a damn mule. If you don't hold it just right it could break your shoulder."

"What's the right way to hold it?" Mark asked.

"Real tight," said Grandpa. "Pull it tight against your shoulder and hold it there till after you've fired."

Mark slid off the trunk and lifted the gun awkwardly to his shoulder. But the heavy muzzle was aimed at a spot of ground only a few yards from where he stood. Then he spread his legs, slid his left hand as far down the barrel as he could reach and strained to lift the gun until it was parallel with the ground. He held it there for a few seconds, until it became too heavy and began to weave. Then he lowered it as slowly and steadily as he could and quietly struggled until he had it recradled in his arms.

"Well," he said, "can I shoot it?"

"Maybe," said Grandpa. "First let's go find another spot. There don't seem to be any squirrels around here this morning. Wait here a minute while I go behind that tree; I'm about to pee down my leg."

Mark watched Grandpa walk across the clearing and disappear behind a huge oak tree. Then he uncradled the shotgun again, grasped it firmly with both hands, lifted it to his shoulder, raised the barrel and began to turn slowly, viewing the clearing over the small sight on the barrel's end.

As his sight swept past the tree which concealed Grandpa, he was startled by a flurry of activity in the fallen leaves. Swinging the barrel back, he saw that the commotion was caused by a large red squirrel burying a nut. By now the gun was swaying badly in his tiring grip. But on one upward sweep he desperately squeezed the forward trigger. Nothing.

Then he remembered the safety, pushed it off and tried again to hold the gun steady.

Grandpa peeked around the tree. As he expected, he saw himself struggling with the gun. "C'mon . . . c'mon . . . you can do it," he said to himself.

He squeezed the trigger.

BOOM!

The recoil from the old 12-gauge knocked him backward and he stumbled over the tree trunk; the shotgun flipped over his head and bounced behind him. As he fell, he saw Grandpa beside the tree, leaning forward, his face twisted, his mouth open. I've killed Grandpa, he thought. I've killed Grandpa. As he continued to fall, the roaring in his head dissolved to darkness.

"Mark!" Grandpa called out of his own darkness. I shouldn't have let him do it, he thought, as he jolted across the clearing. "Mark, boy," he said, shaking Mark's shoulder.

"Grandpa?" Mark's eyes opened quickly. "You're all right?"

"Yeah, but I ought to have my head examined for letting you shoot that gun. Are you okay?"

"I think so," he said, standing and inspecting himself. "But . . . what happened? I-I thought I'd killed you."

"Killed me? You saved my life."

Shaking his head, Mark said, "I don't understand."

Grandpa didn't fully understand either. But he knew he no longer feared what lay ahead. And that was all that mattered.

"What happened to the squirrel?" Mark asked.

CHAPTER 14   THROUGH YOU, NOT FROM YOU

"Last I saw of him, he was running up that tree over there, chattering and whipping his tail around," Grandpa said smiling.

Mark looked at the tree, then at Grandpa.

"Which gun do you want?" Grandpa asked.

"Uh . . . I think I'll do better with my own."

They both laughed as they limped together into the clearing.

Every fear is part hope
and every hope is part fear.

Tom Robbins
Even Cowgirls Get the Blues

CHAPTER 15

when you're finished, you're free

Writing endings, whether the end of a story or the end of a textbook, is as difficult as writing beginnings. The end is your last opportunity to leave an impression on your readers. And you want it to be right; you want to leave the readers satisfied.

At the same time, though, as you near the end of something there's always a strong urge to hurry, to be done with it, because you know that when you're finished you'll be *free* again.

That's exactly the conflict I'm feeling right now. I want this ending to be right, but I want just as badly to be done with it and free from all the restraints that writing this book has placed on me. I'm tired of organizing my thoughts and trying to keep to the point. And I'm tired of editing and rewriting, editing and rewriting. But I have a few last thoughts to share with you . . . and I want them to come out right, so I'm going to try to restrain my urge to hurry.

  ஃ   ஃ   ஃ

Before I start to finish . . . here, this is THE END. You take it.

That's it. Now it's YOUR END. Whenever you've had enough, just stick YOUR END down on the page where you think it belongs. After all, it's your book now.

  ஃ   ஃ   ஃ

Lately I've been thinking a lot about that good old American belief that you can be anything you want to be. I've heard that for years, but now I need to believe that it's true. I need to believe that if I wanted to be a comedian, an orator, a saint, I could . . . by studying and practicing. I don't want to be any of those things, though. I want to be a writer . . . but not a writer of textbooks. Writing textbooks forces my mind to be organized and specific. But I want my mind to feel free to play . . . and to look for the beauty and humor in people and life. I don't want to be straight and serious; I want to be whimsical and eccentric. I need to believe that I can make that change. And I think I've figured out how. (I guess a brain that can find a solution to that problem can't be all bad.) As soon as I finish this, I'm going to work at writing fiction instead of textbooks. And if I ever believe that what I'm writing will turn on lights in people's lives, I'll ask them to read it. If I don't think it will, I'll keep it to myself. It all has value; it just doesn't all have public value.

   🏵 🏵 🏵

Announcer: That was Elton Ego, folks! Wasn't he marvelous!?

   🏵 🏵 🏵

  Many of you are better writers than I am. Or you soon will be. Your writing is intelligent, imaginative, interesting, colorful. You enjoy creating things with words. And many of the things you've created have affected people who have read them. Your creations have made people think and feel . . . have made them more alive, more aware of important things they've been neglecting. Your ultimate goal should be to write things that will make the people who read them more thoughtful, happy, loving . . . more of all the best things humans are capable of becoming.

  Most of you have a rather shaky relationship with writing. You write when you have to, and sometimes you even enjoy it. But because writing doesn't give you the kind of satisfaction you're looking for you'll continue looking until you find something that does. I hope you find it. But don't write off writing completely. If you ever have a real reason or need to write, you'll learn how. That's like a line I heard Tom Waits sing this afternoon: "I never heard the melody till I needed the song."

   🏵 🏵 🏵

  Well . . . I've explained as best I could how to make your writing interesting and effective. I've tried to help you become more confident of your ability to write. I've tried to help you develop a style that is both natural and clear. I've encouraged you to be more conscious of language. I've tried to make you a better reader, by giving you an idea of what goes into good writing. I've suggested that you look at nature, yourself, other people to find what's interesting and valuable in them. I've encouraged you to stand naked . . . to take risks and push out your limits . . . to get into anything, even writing, because it will help you grow. I hope, if you needed to be, you were affected by some or all of this.

If you didn't need to hear any of what I've had to say, I hope you don't regret coming along for the ride.

❀ ❀ ❀

Repeatedly in this book, I have quoted from a novel called *Even Cowgirls Get the Blues*. The author, Tom Robbins, is a friend of mine, though we've never met. (That's a relationship I have with all my favorite writers.) Here's one last thought from him that relates to some of what I've been saying in this book:

> I encourage everyone to take chances, to court danger, to welcome anxiety, to flaunt insecurity, to rock every boat and always cut against the grain. By pushing it, goosing it along whenever possible, we may speed up the process, the process by which the need for playfulness and liberty becomes stronger than the need for comfort and security.

❀ ❀ ❀

Well, that's about all that's been on my mind tonight. And now that that last period (.) is in sight, I'm feeling FREE. Writing this book has taken too much out of me. I've slept too little, smoked too much, overworked my brain and neglected my body. And it's kept me away from too many things I'd rather be spending my energies on . . . my family especially.

Hi, Suzi. Hi, Bridget, Matt, Jude. I'm back.

Oh, I almost forgot. . . .

A Solitary Bird . . . Epilogue

I gathered in my parachute and started walking toward the office, about fifty yards away. As I climbed over a fence stile, I glanced up and saw a jumper whose chute had just opened. Something fluttered in my chest.

As soon as I reached the building I placed a collect call to Suzi.

"Hello?" Her voice sounded tense.

"Hi," I said. "I'm not dead. I'm not even hurt. Man, that was really a trip!"

"You liked it, huh?"

"Yeah, I really did. But it scared the hell out of me, too. It's a good thing I didn't know what I was getting into or I never would have done it."

"Well, what's next? Niagara Falls in a barrel?"

"Naw, I think this'll hold me for a while."

After we said good-bye, I went out to see how the others were doing. As I looked up and around for them, I noticed that it was nearly dark. Then I spotted the last of our group, Gary, drifting close to a large tree, almost half a mile off target. He didn't land in the tree, but he grazed it on the way down to what looked like a hard landing.

Then a couple of the others, grins flashing in the dim light, walked up to the building. Glen, the bartender, was struggling over a fence about 200 yards away. I walked out to give him a hand.

"What's the matter?" I asked.

"Uh . . . I'm worn out," he gasped. "I landed about ten fences from here.

His usually merry eyes were sagging; so was the rest of him. With his long hair, beard and large torso, he reminded me of a buffalo about to collapse to its knees from exhaustion. I relieved him of his equipment and we walked slowly back to the building.

When we arrived, everyone was there except for Gary. The others pointed to him, limping toward us across a field. While someone went to help him, the rest of us exchanged animated descriptions of our jumps. All of us had enjoyed it, but only three were entertaining serious thoughts about doing it again soon: Randy and Danny, the wired-up electrician brothers; and Scott, one of the reporters. All three were gung-ho types, so their desire to jump again was predictable, even though Scott was limping and claiming that he'd probably boken a bone in his foot.

Gary finally limped up to us, in obvious pain. He was pretty sure he'd sprained an ankle, but I doubted it was that serious because I'd just seen him walk half a mile. We learned later that Scott, who thought he'd broken his foot, had merely sprained his ankle. And Gary, who thought he'd sprained his ankle, had broken six bones in his foot. This caused me to reflect on how easily I could have rebroken my leg, and I began to seriously doubt that I'd ever jump again.

(Maybe that's why I'm writing about it: We write about those things that are important to us and that we know we'll never experience again. And we know that even if we were to attempt to repeat them, it wouldn't be the same.)

The last thing we did before leaving was gather around the jump masters to be graded on our jumps. My report read: "Good exit . . . *inverted arch* . . . did not pull dummy rip cord." I hadn't fooled him by sticking my dummy rip cord in my pocket, and I felt foolish for having tried. "Inverted arch" meant that I had rolled over and fallen butt first after I let go of the plane. Also, as I mentioned earlier, I didn't land right. In other words, most of the six hours of instruction and practice had been wasted on me; I'd done practically everything wrong. But I didn't care. I had parachuted, and that was all I'd wanted to do anyway.

When the grading was finished, we headed for the cars . . . the nearest beer outlet . . . and Louisville for some food and celebration before returning to Owensboro. But before leaving the building, I begged a graham cracker from the girl behind the desk. I hadn't eaten since early morning, and now that all the tension was past I was hungry.

I soon wished I'd never noticed that box of graham crackers, though. Within minutes of eating that one cracker, I was siezed with a familiar allergic reaction. Ever since I ate a cinnamon donut and threw up on my aunt's kitchen floor when I was a kid, I've had this reaction to cake donuts and almost all

SOMETIMES YOU JUST HAVE TO STAND NAKED

cheap pastries. My lungs constrict, my heartbeat increases, and my throat tries to close. In spite of my efforts to cure myself with excessive drinking and smoking, that was the condition I was in most of the way to Louisville. Ironic, isn't it: I climb out of an airplane and fall half a mile without an injury, but I'm disabled by a graham cracker.

By the time we arrived at the restaurant, I was feeling better, and more than a little drunk. And for the next hour I catered generously to my day-old appetite.

Meanwhile, Gary's foot was causing him more and more pain. And Scott's was nearly as bad. We were trying to decide whether to take them for x-rays in Louisville or wait till we returned to Owensboro, when one of Kula's kids fell and cut his head on the concrete steps of the restaurant.

That settled it. We asked directions to the nearest hospital and left in a hurry. But we were lost after the second turn. Then Randy spotted a police car, pulled up beside it and called to the officer: "We have two men with broken feet and a little boy with a gash in his head! Will you lead us to a hospital?" I wondered what the cop thought we'd been doing as I slid down in the seat, finished my beer and enjoyed the siren escort.

When we reached the hospital, it was after midnight, and some of us were anxious to begin the drive home. So four of us left in one car, while the others remained to take care of our wounded.

It had been a long day. And an important one for me. I had pushed out my limits a bit. As we rolled down the dark highway, I watched the white lines disappear under the car, read the warning signs and drifted into a daydream about Niagara Falls and a barrel.

Make your life
an interesting story
for others to read
and be affected by.

SOMETIMES YOU JUST HAVE TO STAND NAKED

Dear Reader:

Congratulations! You made it all the way to the end.

Now I have a favor to ask: I'd like to hear from you. Really. I'd like to know what you think about this book. What good did it do you? I'm not looking for praise . . . or hate mail. Just your honest opinion of this book's effectiveness.

Write to Me: David Bartholomy, Brescia College, Owensboro, KY 42301

P.S. If you *do* have any praise to offer, spend it on the student writings you enjoyed. I'd love to pass your comments on to them.

A NAKED INDEX